S0-AEC-459

Teen Challenge

☐ Please put me on your mailing list.

☐ Send more information on your program.

☐ Please send information on how I can help sponsor a student in your program.

Name _____

Address _____

City _____ State _____ Zip _____

Teen Challenge

☐ Please put me on your mailing list.

☐ Send more information on your program.

☐ Please send information on how I can help sponsor a student in your program.

Name _____

Address _____

City _____ State _____ Zip _____

THE JESUS FACTOR

by
David Manuel, Jr.,
Donald Wilkerson, and Reginald Yake

Logos International
Plainfield, New Jersey

THE JESUS FACTOR
Copyright © 1977 by Logos International
All rights reserved
Printed in the United States of America
International Standard Book Number: 0-88270-208-4
Library of Congress Catalog Card Number: 77-74795
Published by Logos International
Plainfield, New Jersey 07061

PROLOGUE

The phone rang on a cold, windy afternoon last November, and a man introduced himself as Reginald Yake, director of the Teen Challenge Training Center at Rehrersburg, Pennsylvania. I drew a blank. Teen Challenge I knew, but I had never heard of Rehrersburg.

He had a proposal for a book project: an updating of the Teen Challenge story through what was happening at "the Farm," as the Rehrersburg center was more commonly known. And now I vaguely recalled that Teen Challenge did have a farm out in the country somewhere, to which they sent street addicts who had accepted Christ and were serious about living their lives for Him.

"There's only one thing," the voice on the other end of the phone went on, "we need the book almost immediately to coincide with the release of our film, *The Jesus Factor*. How soon could you begin?"

I told him I would have to pray about it, but if it seemed right, how about the middle of January?

"How about January 2nd?" he countered, pointing out that they needed finished books as quickly as possible. I hesitated before replying. I was just wrapping up work on a two-year project, the deadline for finishing the final editing of which was Christmas Eve. I had been counting on a breather before taking on anything new. But I also knew that God's estimate of how much rest I needed did not always coincide with my own. We left it that he would call back on December 16th, with Don Wilkerson, the director of the New York Teen Challenge centers.

Don Wilkerson, I thought to myself as I hung up the phone—and my mind went back to another November, six years before. I had been a Christian for seven months and unemployed for one, having left Doubleday, where I was an editor for six years, in order to "write books for the Lord." It never occurred to me to ask God if He *wanted* me to write books for Him; I just drew up a list of the most promising ideas I could think of. At the top of the list was a book that would present the Christian solution to drug addiction, and under it was one that would trace the spiritual impetus behind the founding of America—and with enough money to spend six to eight months at writing, I plunged in.

But the research on the drug book, though I learned a lot, seemed to lead nowhere, and after six weeks I had to face up to the reality of what I'd known in my heart for some time—the book had used up a lot of runway and was not getting off the ground. All the doors were shut, nothing was going right, and I had run out of enthusiasm. I was empty—and scared.

Naturally, I blamed God. Hadn't I done it all for Him? And then God, in the infinite patience He shows His newborn children, had gently led me in another direction. It was a course which first saw me give my life to Him (on His terms, not mine), and join a Christian community, become for two years the book editor of a new Christian publishing company called Logos, and finally, a year later, enter into what I had wanted to do from the beginning: write books for the Lord.

One of the things which was instrumental in propelling me into making a commitment of a lifetime of service to Christ, was a book written by an obscure Assemblies of God pastor named David Wilkerson, called *The Cross and the Switchblade*. As I read this example of what God was doing in response to the author's complete surrender of his life to Christ, I could not read more than a few pages before I would be up and pacing, telling God that this was the sort of faith—and life—that I wanted too.

The morning after I finished, I got in my car and drove from our home in Princeton, into Brooklyn, to find Teen Challenge and put whatever editing or writing abilities I possessed at David Wilkerson's disposal. I found 416 Clinton Avenue all right, but where I had expected to find a weather-beaten brownstone, there was a modern, three-story cinder block building. I even drove around the block and came by again, before it dawned on me that ten years had passed since the writing of the book.

Now what? Well, I had made a decision before I set out, and so I walked up to the imposing white structure. Inside, a gracious receptionist informed me that David Wilkerson was no longer directly associated with the center. His ministry had grown nationwide, and the center was now headed by his brother, Don, who at that moment was on the West Coast. "Would you like to leave a message?" she inquired, and, suddenly feeling very foolish, I shook my head. "You're sure?" she asked again, sensing my confusion.

"No, no message," I assured her and hastily walked out the door. Back in the car, I sat for a moment before starting the engine. The work of Teen Challenge was so vital, and I had been so sure that I could somehow be of help to it—but then, come to think of it, I had been so sure that the drug book and the history book had been right too. I sighed and started for home, beginning to understand a little more about submitting one's own will to God's will, and accepting His direction. My spirits brightened as I crossed the Verrazano Bridge, and though I was a little sheepish at my presumption, I was very happy that God was again in charge.

Pausing for my toll ticket at the entrance to the

Jersey Turnpike, I added a mental note to the file marked "Future Indefinite": some day the drug book would pick up where *The Cross and the Switchblade* left off, and would document the success of the Teen Challenge approach.

Now, staring at the phone I had hung up a few moments before, the thought came to me that God must have been smiling as I had written out that list of books long ago. The history book was the one that Peter Marshall and I were just completing, and the drug book, which Reg Yake and Don Wilkerson had asked me to do and which they would bring out before the other was published, was the one at the top of the list. It appeared that God was going to take me up on my offer, after all.

David Manuel, Jr.
January, 1977

1

"FOREMOST IN DRUG AND ALCOHOL REHABILITATION"

The drive from Cape Cod to Rehrersburg takes eight hours, and the sun was just coming up as I passed New Haven. I yawned and rubbed my eyes, wishing that I had gotten a leg up on the trip the day before instead of staying home to watch the Rose Bowl game. But I was making good time, and as I was not due at the Farm until two o'clock, I swung off the thruway to take the old Merritt Parkway down to the George Washington Bridge.

It was a beautiful morning, clear and crisp, with a fresh dusting of snow making everything new—a perfect morning for driving. The Merritt was almost deserted, and already the sun on the snow was bright enough to require sunglasses. Opening my window a crack to let in some of the fresh air and enjoying the sound of the tires on the road and the sparkling scenery passing by, I soon forgot about being tired and again felt the excitement of starting a new project. By way of preparation, I concentrated on recalling all that I knew of Teen Challenge up until Reg Yake's call. Most of my knowledge came from *The Cross and the Switchblade* which now, I realized, was sixteen years out of date.

In 1958, David Wilkerson was pastoring a small rural church in Philipsburg, Pennsylvania, when he got fed up with watching television every night after his family had gone to sleep. He did something drastic. He sold his TV and committed himself to spending those two hours late at night in prayer and waiting before the Lord—every night. It was a difficult discipline and showed him a great deal about himself and his relationship with God. Then one night, while reading a copy of *Life* magazine, the Lord drew his attention to a news story concerning a bunch of teen-age members of a street gang who had been arrested in Brooklyn, and would soon be arraigned in district court. Incredibly, the Lord seemed to be leading him to go there and help them!

None of it, or the events that followed, made any rational or logical sense whatever, yet David was determined to trust God implicitly. And so he followed his leading into New York City, into the courtroom where the boys were being arraigned, and into a photo of the judge expelling him, which made the front page of the *New York Daily News*. The obscure country pastor from Philipsburg was no longer obscure.

David's pride took a fearful drubbing through that incident, and his total commitment was put to its severest test with his friends doubting his sanity and his family acutely embarrassed. But he persevered. And the gang members, knowing that he had tried to help, listened to him as he told them of a way out—*the* Way out. And then God honored his obedience. Gradually, imperceptibly, he began to make headway. He held a street service (his brother Don was there to help him now), when one of the gang leaders who had challenged him, suddenly and powerfully came under the conviction of the Holy Spirit. He allowed David to pray for him, and he asked Jesus to come into his heart. But not Nicky Cruz, who threatened to kill David.

It was an uphill struggle all the way with many pitfalls, but the climax came when David, again being led by his heart and against all head logic, rented the old St. Nick's boxing arena for what would be the first Jesus rally in modern New York history. The arena was packed. The gangs and their girl friends came from everywhere, but especially from the Bedford-Stuyvesant area of Brooklyn, where the city's crime rate was the highest. There was a lot of mockery and pandemonium, but they listened when David gave a short appeal to let the healing power of Christ resolve their enmities and hatred and bitterness. And when he asked if any would stand and accept Jesus as their Lord, there was an uncomfortable silence. Then Israel stood, and the gang he led, including Nicky Cruz, stood up with him—an entire row. That broke the ice, and it broke the ice for the founding of Teen Challenge, too.

The change in Nicky was real. He described it well in his book, *Run Baby Run*, and, before long, there were others being similarly transformed. Now David needed—and God provided—a place to shelter those whom God was calling to join in this work, as well as those who were beginning to respond to the light of Christ.

This was the birth of Teen Challenge, a work that owed its inception to the grace of God, and to one man's willingness to so die out to self that his will could be entirely yielded to God's. Everything they needed had to be provided by God, beginning with their daily bread. They literally had to pray for it, and it was a constant reminder to them how wholly dependent they were upon Him, and how it was His work and not theirs. God blessed their obedience and trust, moving on the hearts of others to provide them with the minimal equipment they needed. It was never easy, and it never came in one big lump. But there was always enough—just enough.

That was the gist of what I remembered from David's book, and I noticed up ahead, against the clear, azure sky, the eastern tower of the George Washington Bridge. I glanced at my watch: 9:50—I would have time to stop for lunch on the way. Approaching the New Jersey side of the bridge, I maneuvered to the center lane to pick up the express lanes of Route 80, though the traffic was so light that Sunday morning that they wouldn't save me any time.

What else did I know about Teen Challenge? Not a whole lot. I knew that the Brooklyn center had obviously grown substantially, judging from my brief visit there six years before. I knew that there were other centers in other cities. And, of course, there was the Farm. And that was about all I did know.

No, that wasn't entirely true, I thought, heading down the off-ramp and onto 287 South. I knew about the Walter Hoving Home. Located on the Hudson River, across from West Point, about one-and-a-half hours' drive north of Manhattan, the home was a Teen Challenge center for "troubled" girls who sometimes came from affluent backgrounds, as well as from the streets. John Benton, the director, had once invited me there to speak, and I had been sufficiently impressed with what God was doing there to write a piece for *Logos Journal*. From that visit I knew that the Teen Challenge combination of love, truth and discipline worked—in some of the most apparently hopeless cases.

The warning sign for 78 West flashed by, and I got into the right-hand lane. Did Teen Challenge's approach to drug addiction work as well as some of the well-known secular programs? How did it stack up against places like Synanon, Daytop Village and Odyssey House? Some background material which Reg had sent me suggested that it more than compared, but my mind went back to my own research, six years before. I specifically recalled an interview I had been granted with the head of New

York's drug abuse control commission.

I had learned then that there were basically three methods of treating drug addiction: chemical, sociological, and religious. The director had explained the methadone maintenance program to me, how this chemical blocking-agent could appease an addict's craving for heroin at a per-addict cost of $1600 a year. This was a small price to pay, he assured me, when one considered that a hard-core addict's habit might cost him well over a hundred dollars a day to support.

The sociological approach was mainly ex-addicts working with addicts night and day, employing the techniques of eyeball-to-eyeball confrontation, group therapy, and psychological regression. The third method was religious conversion, which claimed to give an addict not a change in environment, but a change of his interior point of view.

The director was also unusually candid as he assessed the shortcomings of each approach. The critics of methadone maintenance, he told me, were quick to point out that it was only a control, not a cure, like insulin was for diabetes. In a sense, it was merely the substitution of one addiction for another. (At the time, I had been reminded of Aldous Huxley's prophetic novel of the future, *Brave New World*, in which he described *soma*, the perfected bliss drug which a benevolent government provided to all who wished to stay doped up perpetually. He had written it in 1932.) But methadone's biggest

6

limitation, I had been told, was only then coming to the surface. It was only a control for straight heroin and had no effect on any of the other drugs that were beginning to proliferate on the street.

On the other hand, the sociological methods, which did claim to cure addicts, did not have a very high cure-rate, and of those that were cured, many developed a heavy dependency on the centers where they were cured, and some never could cut the umbilical cord, as it were.

"As for the religious approach," the director had concluded, "there is no denying that evangelical organizations like Teen Challenge, involved in street ministry, are achieving remarkable results." He smiled condescendingly. "But when you bring God into the picture, it is impossible to evaluate those results rationally, and statistics become meaningless." And he held out his hands, palms up, expecting me to agree with him. I merely nodded and thanked him for his time.

Looking back now, as I crossed the Delaware River into Pennsylvania, I could not imagine why I had not picked up on the lead he had given me. But that was before I had read David Wilkerson's book, and perhaps I had thought that the name "Teen Challenge" sounded corny, or that it was primarily a program for kids. I shook my head. If so, it would not be the first time my smug superiority had blinded me to something that God had wanted me to see. I was glad to be getting a second chance.

The sign—"Shartlesville—1 mile"—loomed up

ahead and reminded me to check my watch. It was one o'clock, time for some lunch *and* some sightseeing since Rehrersburg was less than a dozen miles farther on. There are two famous hotel restaurants in Shartlesville, but one was temporarily closed, and the other had a twenty minute wait. I picked up a hamburger in a souvenir store and spent the rest of the hour driving around back roads, admiring old, red brick or stone churches, and generally getting the feel of the countryside. Aside from the fact that everything was coated in silver-white frozen snow and filtered through a sun-dazzled haze (all of which would transform any terrain into a wonderland), the country had an especially good feeling to it—warm, secure, fertile, and timeless. The gently rolling hills somehow seemed to be protecting the valleys and creeks that ran between them, and I imagined that they were lush and green in the summertime.

There was also a sense of permanence and stability in the large, well-cared-for farms, as well as an out-of-the-mainstream quality, as if they were not too concerned by the winds of change and modern times. I had often thought that the feel of a given place somehow had a spiritual relationship, and though I'd never been able to define it, I had that feeling strongly here. Perhaps it was the unusual number of steeples pointing heavenward, two or three to almost every village. Or possibly it stemmed from the knowledge that I was in Amish and Mennonite country, originally settled by

German Christians who merely wanted to live for God in their own way. When William Penn had opened his colony, he did so to all who professed faith in Jesus Christ, regardless of their denomination, and these German Quakers were among the first to accept his offer. And their descendents, judging from the names on the churches, had clung tenaciously to their beliefs. Whatever the explanation, I sensed God's hand over the land.

It was nearly two o'clock, and I hurried to get back on 78, to watch for the sign which Reg Yake said would show the way to the Farm. Had I been looking for a small, homemade sign I might have missed it entirely, for the sign turned out to be a full-sized, professionally painted billboard, inviting visitors to the Teen Challenge Training Center—"Foremost in Drug and Alcohol Rehabilitation."

That was quite a claim, I thought. Would it stand up?

2

GOD'S MOUNTAIN

My first view of the Farm was of a tall hill, covered on the north side with spruce trees, and on top by a series of buildings, the first of which was a green cinder block chapel with a white spire. The blacktopped driveway was clear of snow, for which I was grateful because it was steep and ran straight up the hill.

Following the arrow for visitors' parking, I soon pulled into a vacant spot, got out and stretched. I had been driving pretty much straight through since three-thirty in the morning, and I felt it. Before locking the car, I placed an open road map over the camera and tape recorder on the front seat—I knew they were safe, but there was no point in subjecting anyone to undue temptation. Inside, the staff member on duty in the front office called Reg Yake at home to let him know that I'd arrived, and then informed me that it would be about fifteen minutes before he got there.

The reception area was plain and spare, and after taking a look in the chapel, I sat down in one of the two old rattan chairs. My first impression of Teen Challenge was that they certainly wasted no money on frills. The chapel's exposed beams revealed a roof of stained plywood, and the banks of folding seats were secondhand and looked as if they might have come out of an old movie house. I had an idea that the Training Center was grateful for every piece of used equipment or material that came their way, and stretched every penny as far as it would go—an impression which was subsequently borne out.

The front door opened and in came a man of medium build, on the chunky side, with full sideburns that were turning grey, and a sense of quiet energy about him. I stood up and we shook hands. Up in his office, Reg showed me some aerial photographs of the 225-acre Farm, explaining that the actual dairy farm itself was down off the hill. The spot where we stood now had been nicknamed "God's Mountain" by the first students to go through the program, and now everyone referred to it simply as "the mountain."

We chatted awhile and I learned that Reg had been an Assemblies of God pastor of a fairly large church in northern Indiana, when he had been recruited for his present position. Reg had been instrumental in the founding of Teen Challenge and had been on its board from the beginning. Then, five years ago, when Frank Reynolds, the Farm's first

11

director, had stepped up to become Teen Challenge's national representative, everyone agreed that Reg was the man to take his place.

After waiting for me while I quickly changed into a coat and tie at the staff home where I would be staying, Reg then drove me to his home in nearby Myerstown. That evening we would be going to a meeting at a church in Ephrata, some twenty-eight miles away, where Reg would show the film *The Jesus Factor* for the first time in the local area. In the meantime, while his wife Grace fixed us a snack (in typical charismatic fashion, we would be going out to eat after the meeting), Reg filled me in on Teen Challenge.

In 1961, a year after the publication of *The Cross and the Switchblade*, David Wilkerson presented his board with a crucial need: they no longer had room for all its new converts, let alone the older ones, and they desperately needed a new facility—a "training" center where they could send the men in their program to be "trained up in the way that they should go" (Prov. 22:6). For weeks they scoured New York, Connecticut, and New Jersey, looking for just the right location, but to no avail. Finally, one day in June 1962, David came back to Brooklyn exuberant. He had been preaching in Lebanon, Pennsylvania, and a Mennonite farmer had come up and offered to sell them a farmhouse and sixteen acres in a town called Rehrersburg.

"Who had ever heard of Rehrersburg?" was the general response, according to Reg, and David had shown them where it was—a tiny town of some four hundred souls in the heart of Mennonite country, surrounded by towns with names like Bethel, Iona, and Mt. Zion.

One weekend soon after, when the weather was beautiful, they all drove out to see it. On the land was a hill slightly higher than those around it. They climbed it and stood there, looking out over acres upon acres of new green corn. It was a warm, sultry day with the sound of crickets being carried on a gentle breeze. From where they stood, they could see three churches over in Rehrersburg, and a western ridge of Blue Mountain to the north. Every one of them sensed a strong presence of God there, and David took a twig and stuck it in the ground, as a symbol of what God would plant there. "Lord, we claim this ground for you," he said quietly, and they all knelt and prayed.

But claiming it was one thing, and paying for it was another. Reg later rode with Frank Reynolds into Myerstown to the local bank to see about a loan with which they would buy the farm. "We've got to be crazy," Reg kept saying over and over. "We're not farmers, we're not from around here, we don't even live in this state! And we've got no collateral!" But God did one more of many, many miracles. And the most amazing were yet to come.

When Frank Reynolds gave up his church on Staten Island to move into the old farmhouse, eight ex-addicts from the Brooklyn center moved in with him. Today, the Farm owns 225 acres and leases

170 more, and has a maximum capacity of 130 students. And there are three other such training centers in the Teen Challenge ministry—at Riverside, California, at Cape Girardeau on the Illinois River below St. Louis, and in Wiesbaden, Germany. In addition, there were now fifty-seven induction centers, all modeled after the Brooklyn prototype, but each unique in its own right and supported by friends in its local area. Of these, forty-one are for men and sixteen for women. In addition, there are centers in Europe and the Middle East, in Australia, India, South Africa, Malaysia, and Brazil.

The stateside centers each had their own induction programs of three to four months' duration, after which those inductees who were ready to become students at a training center were transferred. Twenty-eight centers sent students to the Farm, where they underwent an intensive rehabilitation program which included Bible study and vocational therapy, but which mainly concentrated on their learning how to stand in Christ in the countless variety of daily living situations.

A new class of anywhere from twelve to twenty students, depending on the space available, arrived every month, a few days after the oldest class graduated. At full capacity, which was where the Farm was almost all the time, it graduated more than one hundred eighty students a year, and some twenty-five hundred had completed the program since its inception fifteen years before. But at that capacity, the Farm's facilities (and staff, too, I imagined) were extended to the limit. And while there were plans for a new training center in Puerto Rico, I suspected that there would always be two to three times the number of applicants as there was bed space.

Did they take just drug addicts? "Mostly," Reg replied. "According to the government's survey, which you'll hear more about, almost nine out of ten were on heroin when they came to Teen Challenge, although we are now taking more young alcoholics and kids with emotional problems. The thing to remember is that Teen Challenge takes the bottom of the barrel. The survey also found that eighty-three percent of our graduates had been arrested prior to entering the program, and the majority of those on drug-related charges." Reg nodded to add emphasis to what he was saying.

"In other words, the boy who is having problems with rebellion or who has gotten himself into some minor scrapes, can—or should be able to—obtain counseling from his local church. With our ability to provide twenty-four hour residential help, we can pick up where the churches leave off, but we were intended to be used as a last resort, taking guys on whom everyone else has given up."

From the sound of it, the program was open to more than just teen-agers. "We take them at any age—from fifteen on up to their fifties, with the average age in the early twenties. This seems to be coming down a bit as we take in more young alcoholics, and the average age of drug addicts continues to drop."

Did all the students come from ghetto backgrounds? "That pretty much used to be the case, but now that centers, other than those in the heavily-populated urban areas, are also sending students here, we are getting more of a mix. Our motto is that we will help anyone who wants help," Reg paused. "But he must want it."

Grace called us to the table then and I was grateful for the break. Teen Challenge, an international organization . . . fifty-seven induction centers . . . three other training centers like the Farm . . . twenty-five hundred graduates from the Farm alone . . . incredible!

The night outside was icy and cold, with a stiff wind blowing from the northwest. Reg, Grace, their daughter Lorraine, and I all piled into the car and were grateful that the car's heater did its job in a hurry. On the way, I asked Reg about the movie he would be showing. It was in color, three-quarters of an hour long, and had been made by a Christian film production company named Valley Forge Films, headed by Irving "Shorty" Yeaworth. The main purpose of the film was to show the approach—and the fruit—of the Teen Challenge ministry, mostly through the example of what God was doing at the Farm. But it was also to present the findings of a recent independent, government-funded survey, which was completed in 1975. This survey, which cost $172,000 in research funds and was conducted by the National Opinion Research Center of the University of Chicago, showed that eighty-six percent of the students who graduated from the Teen Challenge program were still drug-free seven years later.

Eighty-six percent?

"Actually, we don't like to use that figure," Reg conceded. "It's so high that it's hard for people to imagine. And besides, that's by the generally accepted standards. According to them, a person is considered drug-free even though he might drink a six-pack of beer a week, or seven shots of whiskey, or a bottle of wine—'social drinking,' in other words. In addition, he can smoke all he wants, and can even use marijuana two or three times a month." Reg laughed. "Our own standards are a little stricter: no smoking, no drinking and no drugs—ever."

I hesitated before asking the next question. "How many of your graduates fulfill those requirements?"

"Only seventy percent."

Only seventy percent! I wondered how the secular programs stacked up against Teen Challenge's. By society's more relaxed standards, a few of the secular programs claimed that sixty to eighty percent of their patients were drug-free at the time they completed their programs. (By that criteria, I thought Teen Challenge could claim 100%.) Apparently no followup had ever been done, either by the secular programs themselves or any independent organization, to determine how many had stayed drug-free after several years. I remembered that the unofficial estimate I had been given when I was doing my own research was ten to fifteen percent.

With those kinds of results, why weren't addicts who were sincere about wanting to get off drugs beating a path to Teen Challenge's door? "Many *are* interested," Reg replied, a little sadly, "until they hear that it's a religiously oriented program—the Jesus factor. Then they shy away and don't want anything to do with it."

We pulled into the church parking lot half an hour early, but there were already a number of cars parked with more turning in behind us. Inside, the church was filling rapidly, and I noticed a number of women wearing what appeared to be little black or white caps on the backs of their heads. "Mennonites," Grace said, in answer to my unspoken question.

"Mennonites? In a charismatic church?"

"They're probably friends of the Farm," Reg explained. "God knew what He was doing when He planted us in the middle of Mennonite country. These people certainly have the love of Christ flowing through them. You wouldn't believe all the ways they help us—produce, hay, farm equipment—why, one farmer even tithed his corn crop to us!" He shook his head. "Those who have come to know us, know that the Farm is doing God's work, and they want to help." His voice trailed off. "What a blessing they are!"

18

Reg turned his attention to the business of threading the film into the projector, and in a little while the lights dimmed and the movie began. From the opening credits, I was impressed with the caliber of production—the cuts and transitions were smooth and logical, the camera-work was imaginative without being obtrusive, and the editing had given it a flow and pace that made me look forward to seeing more work from Valley Forge Films.

The film opened with a good introduction by Chuck Colson, showed briefly what happened at an induction center, and moved on to the Farm, where it captured the spirit of the place by focusing on the people—at work, at play, and in worship. There was also footage of the survey actually being conducted and its results, prefaced and concluded by Catherine B. Hess, who had been in charge of the Pennsylvania Department of Health's drug programs before undertaking the supervision of the survey. Dr. Hess was a fellow of the American College of Surgeons, certified in obstetrics and gynecology, who had taught at the Columbia University Medical School and had initiated the first methadone clinic in the country. Her categorical endorsement of the survey's findings made a strong conclusion to that part of the film.

The closing scenes were of a class graduation in the new gymnasium with more than five hundred guests present. The Farm's choir sang, and then Reg called the members of the graduating class forward, one by one, to receive their certificates, telling a little about each one. As each name was called, a great cheer went up from all the other students, because another ex-junkie, ex-loser, had made it and was about to go forth into a new life in Christ. To those who were just beginning the program, it was a shining promise, and to those in their second to sixth months who might be having a hard time, it was a tremendous encouragement. That one scene seemed to sum up what the Farm was all about, and I regretted that I'd arrived a few days too late for the most recent graduation.

When the church lights went up, people were laughing and talking, and a number came over to Reg to congratulate him on the film. Reg made some closing comments, an offering was taken, and we left to have a late supper at the truck stop in Frystown, the only place that was open all night. I was looking forward to it, not just because I was hungry, but because Don Wilkerson would be joining us. He had stopped off to spend the night on his way back to the Brooklyn center, and I was frankly curious as to what he would be like. I felt I knew a little about his brother from his books, but Don was an enigma.

And so he remained, even after I had met him. Tall, lean, and brooding, with curly, black hair and dark eyes behind horn-rimmed glasses, he spoke with a sort of urgent hesitation that reminded me of Jimmy Stewart. He had a sense of compressed energy—and impatience. I suspected that Don did not suffer fools gracefully.

We had left off Reg's daughter and been joined by Ken Isom, one of the Farm's four division heads, in whose home I would be staying. The table conversation dwelt mainly on the making of the movie, and Reg related how Shorty Yeaworth had initially been stumped by the assignment. "He said there was no way he could make a movie about a bunch of buildings or statistics. And then it came to him: film the people."

Everyone ordered half a chef's salad, and I followed suit, wishing that I had had the temerity to order a whole one. But when the salads arrived, it turned out that the trucks on 78 were apparently driven by jolly green giants—half a salad was the equal of two in most restaurants. I was just debating whether I should try to finish mine, when out of the blue Don said to me, "You saw how the movie caught the spirit of the Farm. We want your book to do that, too."

"So do I," I replied, with more conviction than I had. And I felt the first touch of the icy grip of fear in my stomach. How on earth was I going to capture something that was so easy to see and so hard to put down on paper?

Later that night, alone in the guest room at the Isoms', and dead tired from the drive and all that had happened since my arrival, I lay in bed staring at the darkened ceiling. The "Old Boy" was giving me the gears, as my Canadian friends used to say. He was showing me all the reasons why I couldn't possibly write the book that I had so readily agreed to do.

21

How could I make the story of Teen Challenge's ministry readable? How could I breathe life into the results of a survey, however dramatic they might be?

Satan had all the questions, and I had none of the answers. As I lay there, beginning to doubt everything, I felt that icy hand in my stomach closing into a fist. I knew who was the author of that paralyzing fear, and I told him to buzz off, but in the darkness of that little room, the words had a hollow ring.

3

PEELING THE ONION

On those mornings when one occasionally wakes up before the alarm clock goes off, there are often a few moments in which the body has not begun to stir, and a mind normally given to rapid turning is still at rest. Some Christians are able to attain this attitude at will, through prayerful meditation. But for the rest of us, God will sometimes take advantage of those pre-waking moments to tell us certain things we need to know. As I lay in bed that Monday morning, the movie's solution came back to me—don't show the buildings, show the people.

In that moment I knew that this was the way for the book to go, too. I would be spending that morning with Don Wilkerson so that he could give me the background of Teen Challenge and go over its philosophy, or theology, as he preferred to call it. After that, I was on my own.

No, not entirely on my own. For I knew now that I

was going to have to entrust each day to the Lord and count on Him to arrange whatever would happen. All I had to do was stay out of control and pay close attention in each instance to what it was that He wanted me to see.

Promptly at eight, Reg stopped by to pick me up, and he and Don and I went out to breakfast. After we had ordered, Don looked at me and said, "You know, sin is like an onion. Just when we think we've finally seen it all, the Lord peels off another layer and shows us that there's more we need to see. In a sense, that's what happens at Teen Challenge. When an addict accepts the Lord, for the first time in his life he experiences relief from the guilt of sin. It blows his mind! He's forgiven! Washed clean by the blood of the Lamb!"

Don frowned and traced the edge of his knife with his thumbnail. "But after a while, he gets heavy again. Because now the time has come for him to face up to and deal with his *sins*, plural. Now the Lord would have him see his fallen nature—who he is, without Christ—so that he might be freed from the guilt and bondage of many sins, and be able to recognize them and stand against them in the future. Hence, the peeling of the onion."

But didn't that open Teen Challenge to criticism of being introspective, or putting its students under condemnation, or of just generally lacking joy? Don looked out the window. "Anyone can make a joyful noise unto the Lord, whether he feels it or not," he said at length. "But true joy is a spontaneous thing, a

24

surprise gift from the Holy Spirit. And it often comes after one has seen some new light about himself and realizes anew how much Jesus loves him. The more light a person has, the quicker he can come out of himself and get back into Christ when he happens to do something wrong or something bad happens to him." Don chuckled. "If you want to see joy, just spend some time around any of the centers. I think you'll be surprised."

There was one other criticism that I suspected had been leveled against Teen Challenge. I was remembering how highly structured the life was at the Walter Hoving Home, and the key role that love, in the form of discipline, had played in it. What about the discipline? Reg had even said that there was a half hour of compulsory prayer in the chapel for each student.

"In the beginning," Reg explained, "we have to legislate righteousness for the students, until it is written in their hearts. When a student first comes to an induction center, his conscience has been dead for so long that it is a major victory just for it to be resurrected. Basically, a drug addict has suffered what you might call spiritual deterioration of the spine. In turning to drugs, he has opted for passivity, and he has become spineless. Our job is to develop some Christian backbone in him, so that he can stand on his own two feet. When he goes back into the world, he'll no longer be able to lean on his pusher or his peers for support. The only one he will have to lean on is the Lord."

"When the guys come to the induction centers," Don added, "they're like children who have been stuck in their rebellion for a long time. So they have to be regulated like children till their consciences become fully awakened and they begin to want to set their wills to doing the will of God. When that happens, they are more or less ready to come to a center where they will receive training in how to respond in Christ to almost every conceivable life situation. The more freedom and responsibility that they show they are ready for, the more they are given in anticipation of that time when they will be on their own, with God."

Before we turned our attention to eggs-over-easy, toast, and coffee, Reg had a final comment. "Going from an induction center to a training center is a little like going from high school to college. It's a big adjustment. But the guys have an expression here for when they are having a hard time of it—they say that they are going through tribulation or are being tribulated. You know that a guy has turned the corner when he says, 'I've just seen that *I* am the tribulator!' "

A half hour later we were back in Reg's office, and now Don filled me in on the beginnings. "One of the ironic things is that David did not know what a drug addict was when he went to New York. He went to work with street gangs," Don smiled as he remembered those early days, "but when the gangs became drug addicts, suddenly we had a whole new problem on our hands."

He thought for a moment. "That made it all the more obvious, though, that it was the Holy Spirit who was developing our program, and it was amazing to see how He anticipated the needs of the individuals we were trying to help. After we had worked out the induction and training phases of our program, we began to look around at some of the long-established secular programs and found that they were, in essence, doing the same thing we were."

The center in Brooklyn sprang out of such a need. Originally, they had not started out to have a residential program; 416 Clinton was merely to be a place to house their first workers—"street soldiers" David had called them. But as drugs began to infiltrate the gangs and gradually dominate the street, the workers had to have a place to bring the addicts they were praying for.

Don readily admitted how naive they had been at the outset. He and his brother had been brought up to believe that all a person needed was to be saved and filled with the Holy Spirit, and so they were having the addicts kneel with them on the street and give their lives to the Lord right there. And they would even take the addict out with them the very next day to help with the evangelism.

Sometimes, the Lord *did* spare an addict the excruciating agony of detoxification as he came off of his habit "cold turkey." In fact, this happened often in the beginning, and was God's way of drawing attention to a new work of His, as well as being a tremendous encouragement to the workers. Word of "the 30-second heroin cure" spread through the streets like wildfire. But as the work became established, and the workers matured, more often an addict would have to go through the ordeal of withdrawal with only his new-found faith and the prayers of his new brothers in Christ to sustain him.

It was normal, in the early days of the center, to have thirty-nine workers going out each evening, and one person staying behind to tend the ten or so ex-addicts who were drying out. "But we would come home," Don said, "to find only nine left, and the next night eight, and the next, seven. We came to realize that it was not enough to have them kneel and accept Christ, if we were not going to care for them and give them a real chance." He stopped and looked at me. "In short, we found that evangelism without discipleship was not true evangelism."

Don admitted that he personally loved to evangelize, to go to a place and preach, have an altar call, and minister to those who came forward—instant results and almost always gratifying. And any sticky, ongoing problems in the congregation were the responsibility of the local pastor. But as Don began to travel like his brother David, carrying the message of Teen Challenge further afield, he became increasingly convicted that the call upon his own life was to stay home and assume responsibility for the continued spiritual growth of the center's new converts.

One verse in particular convicted Don. It was Paul's admonition to the Corinthians—"You have ten thousand instructors but not many fathers," (1 Cor. 4:15). At twenty-two years of age, Don was being called by God to be a father to the center's ex-addicts. There was no question in his mind that his brother was being obedient to *his* call and fulfilling that for which he was anointed, but he knew that to himself fell the responsibility for carving out a workable, day by day program. And even so, it was David who usually got the vision of the next major step that they needed to take. Like the Farm, for instance.

"In the early days, David ran into a lot of resistance when he tried to tell people how bad the situation was in New York City. People would simply not believe him and would accuse him, politely, of exaggerating for effect. So he decided to make a movie, showing the drug scene exactly the way it was. Thus one afternoon we persuaded a couple of addicts to take us to their 'shooting gallery' and let us film them actually shooting up. They all knew us and trusted us, even if they weren't ready to buy our message, and they agreed." Don smiled and put his hand over his eyes at the memory of what had happened that afternoon.

"We went up on a rooftop," he went on. "It was a clear, warm summer afternoon, and you could see across the Manhattan skyline. There was no wind, and I remember thinking it was very peaceful up there. Well, as the guys prepared their cooking fire, over which they were going to mix the heroin with water in a spoon, David began to film. Wrapping tourniquets around their arms to make their veins stand out, the addicts brought out their old dirty needles, filled them from the mixture in the spoon, and plunged them into the biggest veins they could find.

"Suddenly, there was a crash behind us, and we all looked up. My brother, who had never actually seen an addict shoot up, had just keeled over!" I laughed, but I also wondered if the same thing might not happen to me.

"When David came to," Don continued, "he stood up slowly and for a long time he said nothing, just stared out at the Manhattan horizon. Finally, he turned to me and said, with as much force as I've ever heard him use, 'We have *got* to get the guys who come to us for help out of *this*!' and he stretched his arm out over the dreary horizon. 'They have *got* to have a chance!' And that," concluded Don, "was the beginning of the Farm."

As soon as the Farm was operational, the Brooklyn center began sending its ex-addicts to it the moment they had dried out. But in many cases, the change was so drastic that the fellows were not ready for it. At the same time, the Brooklyn staff had not yet realized that discipline was actually tough love. But by 1963, it had become obvious to Don that "the guys were running the program; we weren't," so he called a meeting and announced that from then on, the program was going to be run God's way.

What evolved was a three-phase program. First, there was the pre-induction phase, during which most of the guys who were going to leave left; then, a three-to-four-month induction phase, for those who had committed themselves to the full program; and finally, the eight-month training phase at the Farm. The Farm's program was sufficiently flexible so that if a student needed an extra month at the end before he graduated, he could stay on. There was also a three-month "trainee" phase for any graduate who wanted to stay on and work at the Farm.

One of the greatest problems they had with newly arrived ex-addicts was getting them to stay in reality. In his old life, an addict's instant response to the pressures or hurts of reality was to retreat into a state of unreality or fantasy, with the help of drugs if they were available, or daydreaming when they weren't. Thus, when an addict entered the pre-induction phase, he was often in a cocoon of fantasy, a euphoric world of his own making which cushioned and protected him from the slings and arrows of outrageous reality. He did not want God or anyone else reaching in there and touching him, and so he went to great pains to maintain the walls he had carefully built up around himself.

"It's beautiful to watch the Holy Spirit's progress in taking those walls down!" Don exlaimed. "In the first services, a new guy will sit in the last row in the chapel. But as he starts to open up, he will

31

begin to sit farther forward, two or three rows at a time." Don chuckled. "I call it the Holy Spirit push. By the time he's sitting in one of the first three rows, he's ready for the program."

But even after an inductee had accepted Christ and entered the program, the temptation to escape from reality remained strong, and the pattern of avoiding human relationships for years was not easily overcome. Indeed, it may have been the pain of human relationships, or his inability to cope with them, which caused him to turn to drugs in the first place. Thus, despite the fact that he was a new creature in Christ, the inductee might strive to maintain distance between himself and others, either through obvious aloofness or behind a deceptive front of wisecracking or camaraderie. Either way, the last thing he wanted to do was come from behind his mask and be real.

But the Holy Spirit had the answer for that, too, and in the Brooklyn center Don was led to institute what he referred to as Light groups. LIGHT stood for Living In Group Harmony through Truth, and the guys in the induction phase were divided into groups of eight or ten. Each group would live together as a unit with a staff member—working together, eating together, studying together, worshiping together, and going on trips together. And working out their problems together.

In such close proximity, problems would invariably arise, and when they did, they became learning opportunities for all, a chance for each person in the group to see a little more clearly who he really was—and thus, how much he needed Jesus. And as the onion was peeled, each of them began to understand that *he* was the greater sinner. With this revelation came a desire to want to live in absolute openness and honesty with the others in his group and a willingness to trust Jesus and speak truth that needed to be spoken.

Understanding usually grew rapidly after that. Like the insight that correction was not rejection, but love—someone caring enough for his brother not to let him stay stuck in a sin which he was blind to, even if his brother might give him some flack about it. Or wanting to have a mote taken out of your own eye so badly that you don't care if the fellow taking it out has a beam in his. In other words, wanting the light enough to be grateful for it, no matter how unlovingly it might be given or how great the same sin might be in the speaker.

Eventually, the group would reach the point where they put such a premium on living in the light that they would bring real pressure to bear on any of their number, who might be "fronting it," to "get real." Nor would they sit by and let one of their number slip down into fantasy. They encouraged him to choose reality, and walk through the hard places with Jesus.

It usually happened that somewhere in the third or fourth month, an individual really came to grips with the reality of his sin, and around this time he would be a candidate for going to the Farm. At this point, the other fellows in his Light group would indicate, by secret ballot, whether they felt that he was ready. The staff had the final say, of course, and they would be weighing many things—how well the candidate had applied himself to his work assignments and studies, how he had responded to authority, and so on. But they tended to give a fair amount of weight to the peer evaluation, because these were the guys who had been living with the candidate. If he had been "gaming" (treating the whole thing as a game) or "programing it" (just going along with the program), they would know it, where a staff member might not always pick it up.

Going to the Farm meant a tremendous change for the student. Where, at the induction center, he was one in ten, now he was one in 130. On the other hand, where the staff attitude had basically been, "We don't trust you because you have not yet earned our trust," now the attitude was, "We trust you." Reg emphasized that the trip to the Farm was often a very deep experience. Some came fearful; others likened it to going to paradise. "This place is *not* heaven, I tell them in orientation," he said, "because if they come on a spiritual high, along about the second or third month they are going to have an awful fall. But I go on to tell them that neither is the Farm hell. It is a place where they will come to know themselves, and Jesus as their Lord and Master, as well as Savior."

I noticed Don looking at his watch, and I turned the subject back to the induction centers, as I had

some new questions. Were all the centers basically the same? Those in the major urban areas—Los Angeles, Washington, D.C., Miami, and San Francisco—were similar to the Brooklyn center, but those in smaller cities and towns did not have to work with the same raw, ghetto mentalities, and often their inductees would be ready to come to the Farm sooner than four months.
months.

Reg had mentioned that they seemed to be getting more and younger alcoholics now; were there any other significant changes in the guys coming to Teen Challenge? "The street is always changing," said Don, "which is why we have to remain flexible and ready to change ourselves. We can't let our programs start controlling us. In the early days, the moment I thought I finally had the answers, they started asking different questions."

Typical of the ongoing change in the streets was the rebirth of the gangs. Started as a protection against roving addicts who were creating mayhem to support their habits, these new gangs provided a substitute for a sense of community and family that had all but disappeared.

The majority of the guys who now came to the centers for help were poly-drug users, needle and pill freaks who would attempt to get high on anything they could get their hands on. As a result, the number of those with serious mental damage was rapidly increasing, and this presented the centers with their most difficult decisions. Since Teen

35

Challenge was neither licensed nor equipped to operate as a mental institution, for them to take on an individual with a severe mental disorder would be to invite a devastating disruption. "In fact," Don said, "early on, we had to start asking ourselves, regarding guys who were totally flipped out, did the Lord send them, or did Satan?"

"Nevertheless, we are led to take on some pretty far out cases. I guess you could liken it to a field hospital in a combat zone in the middle of an attack. The medical team has to make three categories of casualties: those who are going to live, those who are going to die, and those in between. They concentrate on the last category, and so do we."

Then how much of a role *did* the Holy Spirit play? It was always electrifying to hear of the power of God suddenly delivering an addict from his habit, but there was also inherent in that a temptation to rely heavily on "magic wand" Christianity—the instant cure, the Holy Spirit baptism as a universal panacea for all problems. Quick and painless was the way many Christians wanted it—but apparently that was not the way God was choosing to bring His children into maturity. Increasingly, His way seemed to be the way of the Cross, of going through the valleys with Him, instead of skimming from mountaintop to mountaintop. This was part of the message that David was now preaching, and it explained the emphasis on balance that one found at Teen Challenge.

"An addict *needs* the supernatural reassurance of

the Holy Spirit. He understands it, because so much of his experience has been involved with highs. And so our program is definitely Holy Spirit oriented. The survey showed that in 1968, three-quarters of the guys in the program received the Holy Spirit, and eight out of ten credited Him with having a major effect on the improvement in their performance. *But,*" and here Don stood up, "there's a real danger of going into super-spirituality. And so, one of the basic courses we teach at the center is entitled, 'Fact, Faith, and Feeling.' We make sure that the guys keep them in that order, and are well-grounded in the Word."

Reg smiled. "We have a saying . . . 'too much of the Word, and they dry up; too much of the Spirit, and they blow up.' "

"It's a difficult balance to maintain," Don agreed. "We want to encourage the guys to be sensitive to the leading of the Spirit, but I've also had guys come up to me and say, 'I don't feel saved today.' And mental 'tripping out' is another problem. I'll be preaching in the chapel, and all of a sudden I'll notice that not all of our guys are there. Oh, they'll be sitting there, all right, but in their minds they'll be on a rooftop somewhere in Harlem. Then I'll stop what I'm saying, challenge them on it and tell them to come back into reality—fast!"

The battle of the mind was a constant struggle, and the guys in the program had to learn that fantasy was not a friend, but a subtle and deadly enemy. Here, the Teen Challenge staff was a real help, not just by having a discerning eye for guys who might be tripping out, but by the way they chose reality over fantasy in their own lives. "Most of the teaching is not done in the classrooms or the chapel," Don said. "It is done *in*directly and nonverbally, by example. Most of these guys have not had the sort of mother or father or teacher whom they could look to for a living example of what it means to live in Christ, so they watch us all the time. They learn, not so much by what we say or do, but by who we are becoming inside." He put his hands on his knees. "And these guys can't be fooled. They've had too much experience with phonies not to spot one a mile away."

Teaching by example was one of the keys to discipleship. To new believers who had wanted to know how to live, Peter and John had said, "Look on us" (Acts 3:4). In Antioch, Paul and Barnabas had spent a whole year living with their students, after which the students had been nicknamed Christians. How did they teach? It was Paul who said, "That which you have heard and seen me do, you do, and the God of peace will be with you" (Phil. 4:9). And to the Corinthians he said, in essence, "Here's your assignment: watch me" (1 Cor. 11:1).

Being what Don called a "role model" placed a tremendous responsibility on each staff member, but the biggest mistake a staff member could make was to try to be perfect or hide the fact that he was a sinner. "Whenever you try to cover up a wrong," Don said quietly, "they lose respect for you."

No matter how determined a staff member might be to stay in Christ, he was human, and sin and self were going to come through. But when it did, the key was *how the staff member responded.* As the students saw the freedom that the staff had to be wrong and be sinners, to confess and go on with Christ, it was bound to have an effect on them. Seen from that point of view, the entire day was a living classroom.

It was almost time for us to break, but I had one more question. What about the criticism that the reason the Teen Challenge program was so successful was that the guys who entered the program had come there specifically seeking a religious cure? "The survey told us a lot of things that we already knew," Don said, "but that was one of the few surprises. Of those who dropped out of the program in the pre-induction phase, fifty-six percent considered themselves to have been religious to some degree before they came. Of those who completed the program, only twenty-three percent said they were." He shook his head. "The truth is, it is easier to start from scratch than to overcome religious opinions. And some guys never do get detoxed from religion; they would rather be right and stay in the hell that they have made of their lives, than be willing to be wrong and come into the kingdom."

But what about the guys who weren't really serious? "Sure, we get guys who are coming for 'three hots and a cot,' or they're coming because of parental pressure, or because they know that in a few days they'll be standing before the judge and want to be able to say that they're enrolled in the Teen Challenge program. But God doesn't care; He'll use any of their motivations in order to put them in a position where they have a chance to respond favorably to the light of Christ."

And we got up to leave.

4

"GOD'S PRESSURE COOKER"

The view from the top of the mountain was breathtaking that afternoon. To the east, south and west, gently rolling hills followed one another like billowing waves, all sparkling with melting snow. Behind me, the chapel and the long dorm wing were set into the ridge of the hill, Swiss style, giving a two-story southern exposure on this side, one story on the north side. Directly below me, on the lower level, was a quite large, not unattractive, green aluminum structure which I took to be the new gymnasium, and to the east of it extended a series of large, cinder block buildings with peaked roofs. Although I was curious about them, I suddenly realized that it was getting late and I had much to do.

There were two staff members I had to catch that afternoon, as they would be away from the center for the rest of the week. These were Steve Reynolds and Mel Martinez, two of the Farm's four division heads. The Farm's functions were divided into four divisions—Academic, Counseling, Vocational and Public Service—and Steve was in charge of the first. I found him in his office (if it could be called an office; it looked to be no larger than six by ten feet), trying to tie up all the loose ends before he left.

A bright, earnest, bespectacled young fellow, Steve was the son of Frank Reynolds, the Farm's first director. A graduate of Northeast Bible College, he was currently pursuing his master's degree in religious education, and it was in connection with this that he was about to depart for the Eastern Baptist Seminary. He would be taking an eight-day intensive course on theology in contemporary literature.

I told him what I wanted to see him about. I also explained that I would be happy to wait until he got back—as the present time was obviously inconvenient—but he would hear none of it. "How can I help?" he asked, as I plugged in my tape recorder.

"Well, I don't know a thing, so why don't you brief me on the basics of your division?" And he did.

"Before I begin, I ought to tell you that more important than anything we can formally teach them during their eight months here, are the habits of responsibility that we try to instill in them—being on time for their classes, getting their homework done, coming under the authority of their teachers, making the best use of their study and classroom time, and above all, putting out at all times to the

42

best of their abilities, and to God's glory. If we can teach them these things, then we've given them something that will be of great value to them, whether or not they go on to better their education." (I had already learned from the survey that seventy-three percent did go on to improve their education.)

Given that, Steve went on to explain how the Academic Division worked. Each student had three hours of classes a day, either in the morning or in the afternoon, and the courses were mostly a month long, on an eight-month model. In the first month, for instance, a student would have: Salvation, presenting basic Christian doctrine; Life of Christ, giving the historical facts and background; and English (or Spanish) grammar.

Like everything else at the Farm, the Academic Division had to maintain a high degree of flexibility, for at any given time there could be as many as twenty to thirty students who could not read or write English. This meant that all their courses would have to be taught them in Spanish, while at the same time they were introduced to English. Then, too, there were usually another ten or so who could not read or write at all, and a special class would have to be organized to teach them three hours a day of remedial reading.

"It really gets to me," Steve said, with an edge in his voice, "that some public schools will promote a guy right on up through the system, without ever teaching him to read! And even when I was teaching at a Christian school before I came here, I almost never found a student who was reading at the level he or she was supposed to be at." He spread his hands on the desk in front of him. "But here we can bring them up to a fourth-grade level in three to four months! Of course," he smiled, "they're highly motivated; they want to be able to read the Bible for themselves."

How much education did most of the students have when they came to the Farm? Four out of five, the survey showed, had dropped out of school before finishing high school, and their average grade level was somewhere in the ninth to eleventh grade, although occasionally they would get a student who had gone through college. For those who desired to take their high school equivalency exams, there were G.E.D preparation classes two evenings a week.

In the second and subsequent months, the student studied the Gospels, the Fundamentals of the Faith (Baptism, Holy Communion, Divine Healing, etc.), how to improve his English, a number of courses on the Old and New Testaments, and the practical realities of daily Christian living. There were quite a few courses in this category, though some were only a week long. They included Forgiveness, Relationship to God and Family, How to Study, Money Management, The Christian Home, Management of Time, the Church Relationship, and so on. "You see, it's as I said," Steve concluded candidly, "the classrooms are not so much for formal education per se, as they are for giving a student a new perspective on how to live—a Christian perspective."

Did they have a grading system? The students were graded numerically, and each month their grades were posted. In addition to their academic standing, points were given for their vocational performance, discipleship, general attitude, and gym, and they had to accumulate a certain number of points to graduate. There was even a dean's list for those who had done exceptionally well academically, and there was discipline for those who did not maintain a minimal (and achievable) average—extra work on weekends, and the revocation of all privileges like weekend passes, and so on.

But here, too, they were more flexible than most school systems. "If a guy is really putting out and just can't get it," said Steve, "we'll give him a good grade anyway. But if someone with real ability is just programing it and maintaining a passing average, he will not get the grade he might think he's going to get."

The numerical grades let a student know exactly where he stood, and since everyone else knew, too, they brought certain pressure to bear on him to do his best. An even stronger pressure, in what Steve referred to as "God's pressure cooker," came from another source, a student's own classmates. A class was comprised of those students who began in the same month, and in their third or fourth month, they began to develop a class identity. The students began to care about each other, instead of remaining self-oriented, and they would help and encourage one another, doing all in their power to see that they all graduated together. As a result, fewer than twenty percent had to be rolled back and given an additional month to come into that place in Christ where they needed to be to graduate.

What did the future hold in store for them academically, once they had graduated? "About half of them want to go to Bible school, and about half of those actually wind up going. We've been accused of trying to make preachers out of them, and the truth is a fifth of our graduates do become ministers, according to the survey. Once they come to really see what they've been delivered from and that Jesus is the deliverer, they want to share that, especially when they see how many of their former buddies have not yet seen the light, or think that it's darkness."

Did they have many problems adjusting? "For those going to Bible school, the biggest problem is the shock they get when they find that there is not the same dedication to serving Christ as there is here." Steve grinned. "I try to prepare them by explaining that many of the girls who go to Bible school, go there to find husbands, but even my saying that shocks them."

Nevertheless, those graduates who did go on to school did surprisingly well. Last summer the Farm received a letter from the dean of one of the city colleges of Chicago congratulating them on the record of one of their graduates who had just been awarded one of the college's two Outstanding Student of the Year scholarships. And in the three most recent senior classes presently in the program, of twenty–four students who were interviewed, seven were accepted into Teen Challenge's new leadership training academy at Lindale, Texas. The survey also showed that seventy percent of the 1968 graduates were gainfully employed in 1975. (This figure did not seem that impressive to me, until I stopped to think that zero were gainfully employed at the time they came to Teen Challenge.)

I had two more questions for Steve: what was his greatest frustration, and what was his greatest joy? "My greatest frustration is not having enough time," he answered quickly. Then he thought for a moment and added, "And my greatest joy is seeing a fellow who was having a hard time, make it."

It was after four, and I hurried to catch Mel Martinez, the head of the Counseling Division, before he left. Early the next morning, he would be going with Reg to Puerto Rico for four days of meetings with some men who were interested in starting a training center there, and Mel was to act as interpreter.

The two Counseling Division offices opened into

47

the reception area and were across the hall from the front office, so that they were very much at the nerve center of the Farm. And they needed to be, for Mel and his assistants were responsible for knowing the spiritual condition of every student and trainee at the Farm. It was Mel who approved or denied requests for weekend passes, decided who should go on witnessing missions, who would be the fortunate ones to have a home-cooked meal and an evening of fellowship when some of the local friends of the Farm would offer to have a few of the students over for supper.

And it was Mel who was the head of the discipline committee, comprised of staff members from each of the divisions. In short, if anything went wrong at the Farm, Mel was the first one to be notified; indeed, it seemed to me that he was almost responsible for knowing what was going to go wrong before it actually happened.

Originally from Spanish Harlem, Mel was fairly short of stature, and he seemed to project a quiet forcefulness and a wisdom beyond his thirty-seven years. One sensed that not often did anyone succeed in putting one past him, and yet at the same time, there was also a reflective quality about him that, I imagined, made him someone to whom the students would really *want* to bring their problems.

Another of Mel's responsibilities was assigning bed space to new arrivals and notifying centers that there would not be enough room for some of the candidates whom they would like to send. This he had to do fairly often, and it was at this that he was occupied as I knocked on the sill of his open door. Cradling the phone on his shoulder, he heard my request and held up a list. "We have eight students graduating next month and twenty-one applications," he explained, while he waited for the party on the other end of the phone to come back on the line. "Thirteen guys who are ready to come to the Farm now will have to wait until March, because we don't have enough room." He turned his attention to the phone and completed his call.

Were there plans to expand the center's capacity then? "As soon as we get the new auto mechanics shop finished—that's the building between the print shop and the body shop"—and he gestured to the window behind him, to a just-roofed cinder block structure on the lower level, "we can build dorm rooms in the old garage. We expect that will increase our capacity to 150." He looked down at the pencil he was holding and turned it slowly between his fingers. "And yet at the same time, we have got to retain the personal contact. The last thing that we want to have happen is for the Farm to become an assembly line."

Yet even as it was, wasn't it a little hard to keep track of 130 guys, spiritually and emotionally? The counseling staff received valuable input from the advisor system, I learned. Every staff member had from three to six advisees among the students, and he would meet with them every Friday morning for an hour to talk things over. The students were encouraged to go to their advisors with any minor problems that they couldn't work out with the Lord and one another, and thus were Mel and his staff kept informed of those minor problems which might soon become major ones. Somehow, by the grace of God, it all got attended to, and in retrospect, it was surprising just how much counseling the Counseling Division *was* able to get done.

Did they have any other responsibilities? "Keeping in touch with probation officers and representing students in court is one of our biggest outside jobs." I learned that Teen Challenge had an excellent reputation in the courts, mainly through probation officers who were pleased with their cooperation and continuing positive results. Also, the Farm had a jail ministry to institutions within reasonable driving distance. Mel acted as a sort of chaplain, going two or three times a month, but other staff members and some students went every week.

Did they encounter in their counseling any one problem area more than any other? "Hurts," Mel said quietly. "Childhood hurts that have never been brought to the light, let alone healed. Or ones that hurt too much to bear looking at and were stuffed back down and 'forgotten' about. There are some guys here who have broken hearts and don't even know it—until it's God's time for healing, and the Holy Spirit uses the pressure of the place to bring them to the surface."

Mel was silent for a moment. "A lot of the hurts come out as a result of the living situations that they find themselves in." I remembered what Don had said about an addict tending to wall himself off from others and pad his cell with euphoric fantasies. To find oneself in a room with three roommates, more than likely of different races and backgrounds—a room just large enough to hold two double-decker bunks and a couple of bureaus and chairs—must be quite a jolt. Tribulation of some sort was inevitable.

And a lot of bitterness *was* brought up, with hurt and rebellion usually at its roots. Counseling helped with the former; the program's discipline dealt with the latter. And some of the most fruitful counseling took place when a student met with the discipline committee. By the time a fellow came to the Farm, he knew, intellectually, that rebellion was the sin which caused Lucifer to be expelled from heaven, that authority and "the chain of command" were God's order for mankind, and that submission to authority (as long as it did not force one to go against the will of God) was, in effect, choosing Christ over self.

All this the student knew in his head, but in his heart he might still be smarting from the abuse of authority in his life, or from having no authority figures whom he could look up to. Or it might simply be a matter of sheer willfulness. At a very early age he might have given himself an order that no one was ever going to tell him what to do.

Whatever the source of his rebellion, he now had

to take it on faith that the Lord, by the leading of His Spirit, and through various of His yielded servants, had established the Farm and its program in its present form. He had further to assume that God had brought him here for growth and healing and intended for him to submit to the program. "Nevertheless, not my will but Thine" was a Scripture that became meaningful to the student, and as he did submit his will to God's, and discovered that God honored obedience, he might even find that the job which he was so sure he would loathe would turn out to be enjoyable.

"Lord, change my heart," was a prayer that got quick answers, and as a student reached that point where he could begin to give up his will cheerfully, he found that he could see—and trust—the Holy Spirit operating in the staff's decisions. He could even grasp God's love and mercy in whatever disciplines he might be given. "Whom the Father loves, He chastens," was really true.

The severest discipline of all was dismissal from the Farm, which occurred to perhaps ten students a year, or five per cent, and God would sometimes use this measure as a last resort to turn a hardened or embittered heart. There were instances of students who had been dismissed and who had subsequently had profound changes of heart, reapplied, and gone through the program again with positive attitudes and good results. Mel passed me a letter which he had just received from a student who had been dismissed. There was only gratitude for what the

Farm was doing and what the staff had tried to show him, and repentance for the way he had behaved. "This man learned more from being dismissed," Mel said, "than he did in all the time that he was here."

With a start I realized that we had been talking for nearly an hour. Thanking Mel for his time, I apologized for keeping him so long. He just smiled and said, "No problem."

Later that evening Ken Isom asked a newly arrived visitor named Rick Martin and me if we would like to go with him to a home prayer meeting for the staff, which we did. It was a small meeting of maybe a dozen or so, and we sang some of the familiar scripture verse choruses, then took turns sharing. Using the excuse of my being a visitor, I said nothing, but inside there was more than a little doubt and anxiety. My mind was so full of information that I felt it was like having a bag too full of popcorn in a theater lobby, and now I had to grope my way back to my seat without spilling any.

I could not believe that I had been here only a day and half. If the remaining days were anything like the first, I would be knee deep in popcorn before the week was out. And then, I was supposed to pick only those kernels which—my private litany of woe was interrupted, as I heard someone pray and ask the Lord to sort it all out and show me what He wanted me to see.

I was awfully grateful for that prayer.

5

ON THE MISSION FIELD

There were no peaceful, half-waking thoughts Tuesday morning; the alarm clock went off at seven-thirty like a time bomb, and my feet seemed to hit the floor running. Grabbing my tape recorder, I latched onto Ken as he went out the door. Since he and his family would be leaving Thursday for a month, the only choice I had was to stick close to him all day and go with him wherever his duties took him.

The first place they took him was the staff lounge, where there was a meeting of the staff of the Vocational Division, of which Ken was the head, promptly at eight-thirty. (I was beginning to notice that things took place when they were scheduled to at the Farm—8:30 meant 8:30, and not 8:35, and people made a point of getting to places a few minutes earlier, rather than waiting to the last minute and then running, as I too often did.)

The meeting began with devotions, which was its main purpose, and then there was some division business. The 2:30 A.M. cow-milking shift had not responded to the nightman's call, and a student's indulgent parents had sent him $300 spending money. About the only thing at the Farm to spend money on, other than books, was the commissary, which was open for three-quarters of an hour a night for candy, ice cream, and hot sandwiches. "Man!" said one of the staff. "He's going to have to buy a lot of candy!"

"He's got a lot of friends," offered someone else.

"He's got *all* the friends!" said a third, and everyone laughed.

The meeting broke up a little before nine, when chapel let out, and Ken went downstairs to the "dentist's office." This room, equipped with a used dentist's chair and drills, was occasionally used by a local Christian dentist who donated his services to the Farm. In the meantime, it doubled as the Farm's dispensary, and one a week a registered nurse came to take sick call. The rest of the time sick call was taken by Ken, who was a doctor of veterinary medicine. There were a half dozen guys lined up at the door waiting for Ken, who unlocked it and invited the first one in. I tucked myself in a corner to watch the proceedings. The room had an eye chart, a corner full of secondhand crutches, and a number of cartons of donated supplies—soap, bandages, nonprescription medications, etc. There was also a locked medicine cabinet and the only piece of modern equipment—a hydrothermic sterilizer.

Apparently there was an intestinal bug going around; the first two guys complained of diarrhea. But Ken was equally thorough with each. "Do you feel nauseated?" Negative. "Any pains?" Negative. "Well, stay away from fruit juices, milk, and greasy foods, and I'll have Tony give you some indoor work." (Tony Foret was in charge of General Help, the work detail for all students not assigned to one of the shops.) Ken called the front office on the intercom. "Did my order of Kaopectate come in yet? What, three little bottles? Look, get a gallon of pectacone as quickly as you can; it looks like we may need it. Thanks."

A sprained ankle came in next, a basketball casualty from the gym. It was swollen, but not too badly, and it had not yet discolored. "Does this hurt?" Negative. "Does it hurt when I do this?" And very gently, Ken manipulated the injured foot. "Some stretched tendons here," he said. "I'm going to put on an ace bandage, snug, to hold down the swelling and give some external support, but not too tight; we don't want to cut off circulation to your toes." And he deftly wrapped the bandage this way and that way around the ankle, taping down the end. More and more I was coming to admire this short young man with the round smiling face. "Okay, keep this foot up for the next few days when you're not actually moving around."

In came a bad toothache then, resulting from a cavity which had lost its filling. "But muh whole mowf huhts!" the patient complained when Ken told him what the problem was. "It huhts heah an heah an ovuh heah!" And he gestured in the general vicinity of his mouth.

"That's what we call 'referred pain'—like two wires side by side: when electricity goes through one, the other picks up some of the charge. When the pain sent by an irritated nerve end gets back to a junction, it sends out signals to other parts of the mouth." All the while he was talking, Ken was also mixing a paste of zinc oxide and eugenol and cotton on a small glass palette, back and forth, back and forth. Then he cleaned out the cavity and packed it with the paste. "This is just a temporary filling, but it will hold until the dentist comes. It'll also protect that nerve from further irritation, and give the pain a chance to subside."

"Fansh, Doc, ih fee-uzh behher arready." The patient stopped at the door. "Gah besh yeh, Kenh."

Ken smiled and nodded, his concentration on the file card in his hand. When he finished what he was writing, he looked up, and noting my curiosity, explained, "So the dentist will know what I've done. We keep a card on every guy who comes in here, and add to it the reason for every visit, no matter how insignificant." He put the card in the file. "When a guy comes off heroin, he's not used to hurting, so every little ache and pain, which most people would ignore, tends to alarm him. Most of the time, we'll put his symptoms in a holding pattern and see if they don't disappear. But we never take any chances; the moment we have the slightest suspicion that something might become serious, we call the doctor right away." He held the door open for me. "The key to this job is knowing your limitations." And he locked the door behind him.

When we got to Ken's office, I asked him about his veterinarian training: was it as hard to get into veterinary school as I had heard? He nodded. "Because there are comparatively few vet schools, it actually takes a higher grade point average than it does to get into medical school. But even though the systems of higher mammals are remarkably parallel to those of man—as are their illnesses—it still requires four additional years of schooling to switch from one profession to the other, and a vet would have to spend two more years interning after that."

Had he always wanted to be a vet? "What I really wanted to be was a Christian missionary. I gained an interest in veterinary medicine early on, but it was in college, while I was taking two years of premed, that I began to feel called to some sort of ministry. I finished four years of veterinary school and got my license, and that enabled me to support my new family through the necessary three years of Bible school. I was able to get a job as an associate to a vet with a private practice, and I made $400 a week," Ken chuckled.

"But still, my one interest was the foreign mission field, and I was counting on the veterinarian part to open doors that might otherwise be closed. Nepal, for instance, had closed its borders to missionaries, but urgently needed veterinarians . . .," his voice trailed off, and I wondered for a moment if he might be thinking of a village nestled high in the snow-covered Himalayas, with small, dark-eyed natives tending herds of yaks.

"So the next step," he resumed, all business, "was to get in two years of ministry stateside. I heard about an opening here and came in 1971." He laughed, "It's 1977 now, and I'm still here. And God has not given any indication that He intends to move me. But you know, a curious thing happened just about two years after I came," and he looked at me with his head slightly cocked. "A missionary came through here, and I showed him around, telling him about the ministry of the Farm. When we'd finished, I told him that I, too, had felt called to the mission field. He looked at me with the most startled expression on his face. 'What do you mean, *to* the mission field? Man, after all you've shown me, I'd say you were standing on one of the best mission fields I've ever seen!' " Ken smiled. "After that, I began to see that I was exactly where God wanted me. And now I really feel at home here, challenged and fulfilled." And stretched out flat, I thought to myself, which was part of being fulfilled.

Did he do the Farm's veterinary work? In the beginning he did most of it, but now that their herd had grown to 106 Holsteins and he had accumulated other duties, it was done by a specialist in milk cows, and his own veterinary work was done on an emergency basis. His other responsibilities now required every bit of his time.

I wondered what Ken was being paid then, and after hesitating, I asked him. "Less than half of what I was making while I was going to Bible school. But it's enough for Joyce and me and the two girls. And the center provides our housing and takes care of our utilities. The money may be lean, which is why we haven't been able to beautify the Farm, but no one has ever missed a paycheck."

Ken told me then of one of his favorite projects—the Farm's vegetable garden. Started three years ago, it had grown to where there were now five acres under cultivation. The produce could not yet begin to replace what they bought in bulk for the kitchen, but it made a substantial, nutritious supplement that also tasted good. "Last year, we harvested between six and seven thousand ears of sweet corn, enough to last us for a year. And then, wouldn't you know it, corn turned out to be the crop that people donated the most of. We had corn coming in by the truckload, corn piled high under the trees, corn everywhere, till we got to the point where we almost didn't want to see another ear—" he glanced at the clock on the wall. "But I'll tell you about that after lunch."

It was another beautiful day, almost painfully bright, and what snow was left was melting fast, turning the surface of the driveway a shiny black. I inhaled a deep, tingling breath and followed Ken up the terraced cement stairway, toward the dining room, which was under the dorm but had southern exposure. From Reg I had learned that although the major part of the building program had been the result of continuing support on the part of the Farm's friends, there had been two larger grants: $80,000 towards the new dorm wing, and $20,000 from Kathryn Kuhlman towards the academic wing.

Reg had also told me a story in connection with the completion of the academic wing. Kathryn Kuhlman had come back to dedicate it, and Frank Reynolds and the others had worked to a state of exhaustion to finish it in time for the dedication ceremony. He could barely talk, he was so tired. At the end of her dedication, Miss Kuhlman, in her own inimitable style, raised her hands to heaven and cried out, "O God! Cover this mountain with buildings!" Whereupon, Frank was heard to groan, "O God! Cover her mouth!" I looked around; her prayer was fast becoming prophetic.

In the dining room, lunch was scrambled eggs with bits of pork mixed in, baked potato, buttered corn, bread for those who wanted it, flavored drink and ice cream. The eggs were tasty—and real. I learned that a local poultry farm donated its cracked eggs to the Farm. I also learned that the Farm was given ten *tons* of potatoes last year, and I was reminded of two other memorable gifts of food that Reg enjoyed telling about.

A couple of years ago he had received a call from the Quaker Oats people in Chicago. "We've got 17,000 cases of our 100% Natural Cereal that we want to give away. How many cases would you like?"

Reg had no idea how much cereal that was, but they wanted an answer right away, so he said 5,000 because they said that they would take care of the shipping. It arrived in three tractor trailers. They shared it with every charitable organization they could think of.

Another time, a local friend of the center called and asked if they would like to have eighty bushels of cabbage. "Great," said Reg, and then he wondered how many heads were in a bushel. "About ten," said the farmer, "but never mind worrying about what you're going to do with it all. Come Saturday, my wife and I will come over and turn that cabbage into sauerkraut for you." And they did, working all day and putting it into jars. Only it wasn't cooked quite long enough to kill all the bacteria which began in turn to produce gas. And before long, there was a tremendous *bang* and then another and another, as a few of the jars exploded. And suddenly they had sauerkraut everywhere. "But we are still grateful for *whatever* the Lord brings our way," Reg had hastened to assure me.

The buttered corn turned out to be even better than it looked, but the ice cream had a most unusual texture to it. Mixed in, were strains of a darker, slightly chewy, slightly grainy substance that was familiar, but I couldn't quite place it. Was it figs? No—plums? No— and then I had it! And I couldn't believe it; nor could I decide whether I was glad that I had been able to identify it or not. It was *peanut butter* ice cream! I learned then that it, too, was a gift, and I tried to shame myself for having looked a gift horse in the mouth.

The noise in the dining room, as the students came through the line and filled up the tables, was loud but cheerful, and different from that of large dining rooms in my memory. At college and in the Navy, the decibel level could go up, but when it did, it was competitive noise—one table trying to make itself heard above another. There was another difference: in those days each table—and each individual at each table—was totally absorbed in himself, and the dining halls were very lonely places to be. Which, of course, was the way we self-centered individuals preferred it.

But not so at the Farm. Here, the noise, the kidding, the laughter, was a warm, friendly thing that filled the corners of the room and enfolded everyone. Once immersed in it, you couldn't help smiling. That made me think of what Steve Reynolds had said about the bond that developed between the students and how they strived to help one another, and I mentioned this to Ken.

"It's really amazing, isn't it," he said. "You know, in public school, you take an average class of thirty, and you're going to have one, maybe two kids who are real rebels. Every student here was one of those rebels, and yet we hardly ever have any fights. We have 130 former thieves and almost no thievery." He shook his head. "You ought to see the way new visitors will clutch their purses and carefully lock their cars the first time they come (I winced), and

63

yet hardly anything ever gets taken."

Back in his office after lunch, I asked Ken to tell me about the corn. "Well," he said, stretching back in his chair, "it just kept coming and coming. And we stacked it everywhere we could think of. For days, every available man was doing nothing but husking corn. In fact, we got the entire student body out, directly after lunch and during their free time. Some of the guys griped at first about having to give up their time, but once they got involved, a real spirit of fellowship and camaraderie developed." I recalled what I'd learned in researching the history book, about the early Puritans who got such joy from barn-raisings and harvest-times, any time that they could do such work together. And undoubtedly they had had their husking bees, too. God seemed to have a special blessing for His children when they united in a common task.

"We shucked corn for days and days, but that was only the half of it. Now we had to get it ready for the freezer. (To take advantage of the Lord's unexpected bounty, two years ago the Farm had purchased a walk-in freezer.) This meant blanching it in a big tub, which we kept at a boil with an old army burner. And then we had to cut it off the cob. We had guys cutting off corn on every available table top, and when it was cut, we stored it in old plastic bread wrappers—we save everything, here—then froze it and restacked it. Actually, the ideal containers were old milk cartons with the tops taped flat. Once they were frozen, they could be stacked like bricks and took up the least amount of freezer space."

Ken was warming to his subject. "But if you think that was something, you should have been here in pea-picking time. We put in English peas last year because the guys really like them. But they take forever to pick. And we found that the staff had to pick right alongside the guys to help them to learn to care about what they were dong, and not pick them haphazardly and leave half behind or pick them too green." Ken stopped while we got our coats on; he had a vocational orientation lecture to deliver at one o'clock.

"Fifteen of us picked the entire morning, and then we held the guys in the dining room after the noon meal, and poured pods down each table for them to shell. Their attitude, and the change in it, was a repeat of what happened with the corn. It was a little discouraging to have all that labor consumed in a single meal, but the peas tasted terrific." He held the door for me. "Next year will be different. I found out that you could separate the rollers of the hay-binder, so that it will harvest—and shell—the peas. So we'll be planting a lot more, come spring."

I smiled. It was unlikely that any commercial farmer would then give them a tenth of his pea crop, but you never know.

6

"ACCOUNTABILITY,
RESPONSIBILITY,
FAITHFULNESS . . ."

In the chapel, the lights were darkened for the slides Ken would show with his lecture, and I struggled to fight off drowsiness, my head full of corn and peas. But Ken's opening words took care of that.

"We have one purpose here: to mature in Christ." And he proceeded to enumerate eight qualities which the Farm's vocational training would instill in them, if they gave it their best. These qualities would be of far more benefit to them than any technical skill they might acquire, because they would enable the students to work to God's glory in any capacity or line of work they took up after leaving the Farm.

Accountability—they were going to be held accountable for everything they did. Jesus called them to no less, and their employers would expect it of them wherever they went after the Farm. This meant, for instance, that they were to account for any time spent out of their assigned work areas, such as counseling or getting haircuts. Such absences, no matter how legitimate, had to be approved by the staff member involved. "You can take this two ways," said Ken, as if he could read their minds. "Either as a stringent discipline to put you in a box, or as an opportunity to let it do a work in you and grow in Christ."

Responsibility—they would learn to be responsible; for example, notifying their supervisors if they were going to be absent or late, no matter how valid their reasons. It was gross irresponsibility for them to leave their supervisor in the lurch, and their sudden, unplanned-for absence could hurt others. (I had learned that one such unexcused absence meant discipline, two warranted an appearance before the discipline committee and could result in dismissal.) In the world, being responsible in this way indicated to an employer that the employee really cared about his job.

Faithfulness—there were many ways in which they could demonstrate this quality: by always being on time (and there were time clocks in all the shops so that they could get used to punching in), by always keeping busy, and never missing work unless it was really unavoidable. "A Christian should be the best worker on any job," said Ken, "the top man, known for faithfulness in giving his best."

"But we don't even get paid here," pointed out one of the newcomers.

"Yes, you do," Ken replied. "You get paid your

room and board, your education, and the vocational skills you'll be learning. And most important, you're being taught something about how to live in Christ and go on living in Christ after you leave here. All told, considering what it costs to run the Farm, you're being paid about eight dollars an hour, which is more than most of you have ever made before."

Submission—yielding in opinion, judgment and wishes to those in authority. All staff were to be treated with respect, regardless of their ages or position. And again, there were two ways to take it. Ken suggested that they look at it as "the freedom to be creative under the protection of a divinely appointed authority."

Initiative—seeing and doing what *could* be done, rather than doing only what *had* to be done. And in Christ, it *could* be done without placing one's self over one's supervisor. Initiative was something that they should practice everywhere, and not just in their jobs. "Some of you guys, for instance, who have never sung in your lives, are going to find out that you can sing. We've had non-singers wind up as soloists in the choir, and I would challenge every one of you new students to volunteer for everything, from the choir to working on the farm."

Industry—working to the limit of their God-given abilities, with dedication and zeal. "You'll find, I pray, before leaving here, that the only life worth living is a life that's pushed to its fullest potential."

Stability—continuing to perform at their

potential, regardless of changing circumstances. "Stability is staying on a job that you have become bored with, or otherwise turned off by. Some of you have been real jack rabbits when it comes to holding a job, and so to help you we have a rule here: once you are placed in an assignment, you'll work there for three months. At the end of that period there'll be a review, and you'll be allowed to change your assignment, if you want to. But whatever you pick then, you'll stay in that assignment until you graduate."

Honesty—doing top quality work for the hours for which they were responsible. "You are cheating God, the Farm, and yourselves if you don't put in three good hours at your assignment, every day."

Next, he turned to the training that was available, and it included auto mechanical repair and body repair, carpentry, cooking, custodial skills, dairy farming, electrical wiring, greenhouse work, heating and air conditioning, plumbing, printing, radio technology, and wastewater treatment. Passing out some sheets among them, Ken instructed them, "You'll see where you are to fill out your first three choices of what you would like to be assigned to. Number your preferences next to the jobs, and we'll do all that we can to give you your first or second choices. You'll also see a space to put down any plans or desires you might have for the future. Be sure to fill that in, too, and be honest, because there might be something that we can do to help, either during the program or afterwards."

I wondered, then, how the vocational program had come into being, and it was Reg who later provided the answer. A number of years ago, a student who was about to graduate asked if the Farm could help him find a job. What sort of work had he done in the world?

"Well, when I was in Sing Sing, I worked in the kitchen, and when I was at Chilicothe (the state penitentiary in Ohio), I worked on the farm, and when I was in Lexington, I worked in the bake shop."

Had he ever had a job outside of prison?

"Yeah, for two weeks, but I can't remember what it was."

So the Farm incorporated into its program a division that would concentrate on the practical aspects of learning how to work, and for the completion of which a certificate would be granted, that graduates might show to prospective employers.

Ken called the men's attention to the next item on their sheets. "You will each be evaluated monthly on your performance in the Vocational Division. Everyone's grades will be posted on the bulletin board, and so that you will know what the numbers mean, a '4' is excellent and means that you work well with minimal supervision and exercise initiative. A '3' is good and means that you work well, but do only what is asked of you. A '2' is fair and means that you will do the work but require constant supervision. A '1' is poor. Even when supervised, you avoid doing the work assigned to you. And a 'zero' is intolerable, meaning that you have a generally rebellious attitude. I'll tell you, if you get a '1,' you will probably be dismissed, and if you get a 'zero,' you will certainly be dismissed!"

Next came a rundown of the daily routine: up at 6:15, breakfast served from 6:30 to 7:00, room cleanup and personal devotions till chapel, which ran from 7:45 to 8:50. Beginning at 9:00, there were three 55-minute classes for half the student body, while the other half worked at their vocational assignments, and at 1:00, the two halves reversed. From 4:00 to 5:00, there was rehearsal for those in the choir, and free time for study, letter writing, etc., for the rest. Also, each student had one afternoon a week of assigned gym during that hour. Dinner was served from 5:00 to 5:30, and afterwards there were G.E.D. classes, welding classes, and other voluntary activities or recreation, until the beginning of compulsory study time at 7:30. From 8:45 to 9:15 was compulsory prayer, and from 9:15 to 10:00, the commissary was open. At 10:00, all students were to be in their rooms for personal devotions, and 10:30 was lights out.

At first glance, it seemed like a rigorous schedule indeed, but doing a little calculating, I discovered that a student actually had four and a half hours a day in which he was responsible for deciding how he would spend his time, which seemed a pretty fair amount, all things considered.

The rest of the session was spent in questions and answers, and before long, it was getting on towards

71

three o'clock, when Ken had a class to teach on the Christian point of view. At the pace this day was going, I thought, I could use four and a half hours just to catch my breath.

Taking a brief stretch outside before going on to the class, I noticed an irregular pattern in the cinder block wall of the print shop, like some of the blocks were new or had been replaced. The pattern was roughly the outline of a cave entrance, and I asked Ken about it.

He seemed to wince at the memory. "You see that extension, next to the kitchen over there?" I nodded. "Well that's the receiving dock for our bulk kitchen supplies. One day, a truck backed in there to be unloaded, and someone had forgotten to set the brake or leave it in gear. It began to roll."

"Oh, no!" I exclaimed, looking from the dock, over the edge of the drive and down the hill to the print shop.

"Oh, yes. Before anyone could stop it, the truck had gone over the side and down the hill, gaining momentum all the way. When it hit the wall, it smashed right through it, sending cinder blocks flying in all directions!"

"Was anyone hurt?"

"No, and that was the grace of God, all right. Whoever was in that part of the shop had moved away from that area. We were even able to fix the truck and repair the side of the building, as you can see. But some of the equipment inside got pretty badly damaged."

We went on to the classroom, getting there just at three. There were thirteen guys there, all present and accounted for. The first thing Ken did was pass out some optical illusions, at which the guys (and myself) marveled at lines which we were certain were curved, but which turned out to be straight, and volumes which had to be different, but weren't. Next, he began a filmstrip which had some more illusions, even more surprising.

"All of which goes to show you that you cannot always believe what your eyes tell you is the absolute truth. And that goes for your other senses, as well. You can walk into a room that smells really funky, but after a while your nose has adjusted to it, and you don't notice it anymore. But another guy comes in, and *he* smells it—" here Ken recoiled in mock disgust. "You see, it all depends on your point of view, where you are coming from."

In the same vein, he went on to point out that what was hot to one person might feel cold to another, depending on their body make-up, and again, where they were coming from. And as with smell, what they were really sensing was *change*.

Both our eyes and our ears were really much more limited sensors than we supposed. All we could see, for example, was "visible" light, which was actually a very short part of the light spectrum. Outside of that limited range were infrared, ultraviolet and x-rays. And when it got low enough, the light wavelength

73

became sound. And then, too, there were sounds so low that we could not hear them, but we could feel them. And so high that we could not hear them, but a dog could.

"You would be foolish to say that, because you could not hear a sound, there was no sound. But men have long been saying things just that foolish—that because they cannot see, hear, touch, smell or taste a thing, it does not exist." Ken paused to let the class think about that.

"You know, this room you're sitting in right now is filled with literally hundreds of broadcast waves, each simultaneously carrying its own message. You can't see them or hear them, but they're here. All you have to do is have the right receiver. Turn on an AM radio, and you can hear a number of the broadcast waves in that frequency range. Turn on an FM radio, a shortwave set, a CB, and you can hear more of the waves that are here. Turn on a VHF and a UHF TV, and you'll be able to see pictures that are being broadcast that are also here." There was a murmur in the classroom, as the students responded. I was wondering if they were also thinking that the room was filled with God.

"Did the radios and the TVs *create* the sound and pictures? No. All they did was *receive* and amplify what was already there. If you realize that, then you'll realize how limited your own perception—the input from your own built-in system of receivers—really is. And once you realize how easily you can be deceived, then you can realize, 'I'm not always right.' "

Ken used the example of a good pilot being one who knows that his own perception was so fallible that, whenever he was flying at night or in the clouds, he chose, by an act of his will, to trust only his instruments, regardless of what his senses might be telling him. "Which is one reason why God gave us this, right here," and he held up a Bible. "What this tells us about how we ought to live, plus our consciences and the guidance of the Holy Spirit, are the instruments God intends us to use. If we fly by them, we won't crash. But if we start trusting our heads or what our senses tell us, we're going to get into trouble."

He told them that they needed to tune their receivers to God's example, as put forth in His pilot's manual—solid, immovable, never-changing. If they took their eyes off the instruments and started flying by their own perceptions, they would wind up flying the plane right into the ground.

Now Ken advanced the filmstrip and showed a picture of a man seated behind a desk, talking to another man sitting alongside the desk with his back to the camera, with a third man standing nearby, looking at the second. Then he asked for someone in class to tell him what was happening—the first thing that came to mind. One student saw the situation as a job interview, another as a session with a probation officer, a third thought it was a kid in school who had gotten into trouble and been taken into the principal's office by the teacher (standing).

"The point is," said Ken, "you're going to interpret a situation where you have very few facts to go on, by your past experience and what you might have been thinking about at the time. If I had been talking about job interviews shortly before showing that picture, everyone of you would have been conditioned to come up with the first answer. It's natural, but that does not necessarily mean it's correct. What *do* we need for a correct interpretation?"

"We need to hear the words," said one.

"We need to see the face of the guy sitting down, to see if he's getting yelled at."

"What we're basically saying," concluded Ken, "is that we need more information. Which is a good reason for never jumping to conclusions or prejudging a situation."

He advanced the filmstrip again. Now there was a picture showing a body lying still in a road by a curb, with another figure bending over it. Though it was broad daylight, the sun was so bright on the green hedge beyond the curb, that the two figures in the foreground were in silhouette, so that it was impossible to make out exactly what was going on. Nevertheless, there were some strong, immediate reactions. Several hands shot up, and Ken said, "One at a time! Okay, what's happening here?" And he pointed to one student with his hand up.

"That guy lying down got shot by the police, and that's the policeman who did it, bending over him. Because if it wasn't a policeman who shot him, whoever did it wouldn't be hanging around. He would have kept on running."

"Okay," said Ken, "someone else."

"I thought it was someone bending over the fellow lying down, to see if he could help him."

"To me," said a third, without waiting to be asked, "the guy bending over has just stabbed the other guy, and is pulling out his knife, or going through his pockets."

Ken motioned for quiet. "Now, what if, just before showing this picture, I had added these sounds," and he imitated the noise of a car being driven fast, the squeal of tires, and a thud. Everyone went "oh," and then chuckled.

"The point again is, don't leap to conclusions. *Don't* be dogmatic, or bound by your opinions. Don't get locked into seeing something—or someone—one way just because you've been conditioned to it. And don't remain convinced that that's the only way to see it, before you have all the facts."

Ken announced their homework assignment for the next day: they were to write at least a half page telling of a situation in which they had had conflict in their own lives because of a differing point of view. How had they handled it, and then, looking back on it, how should they have handled it?

"Keep in mind that you see what you want to see, or what you're conditioned to see. On a long car trip, I'll notice all the veterinary hospitals that we pass, where someone traveling with me might not see a one. A hungry man looks at an apple tree and sees a source of food. A man who's hot from the sun sees it as a place of shade. A lumberman might see it in terms of how many board feet it would yield. A botanist would notice if it had rust or spots on it. An artist would see the beauty of it." He paused. "Each man would see it differently, and yet it's the same tree."

Ken smiled as he thought of another illustration. "Or take taste, for example. One man's delicacy might be another man's poison—in Africa, they eat insects. And then there was the lady missionary visiting a Navaho reservation, who was invited to have a bowl of soup. She liked it and was dipping the ladle into the pot for another, when her hostess said, all smiles, 'Dig deeper, there's puppies in the bottom.'" There were groans and then laughter, until Ken said, "Bring it back together, men. We only have three minutes left."

Those last three minutes were spent in review—we cannot and should not trust our own senses exclusively. We need God's input and need to trust His guidance system rather than our own. We need to be leery of our own tendency to form conclusions before we have enough facts to go on. We need to see that our prejudice—our prejudging of a situation or individual—is the product of our own conditioning and of where we are coming from. And therefore, it is not to be trusted, because we have seen how often our opinions, our own point of view, can be wrong. "Our point of view is the sum of our attitudes. And the thing we deal with the most, here at the center, is attitudes. Christ saves us, and that's an instantaneous thing. But changing our attitudes—that takes time."

Prejudice was a point of view that was set. There was an incident which Reg Yake was fond of relating. A new student arrived at the Farm from Birmingham, Alabama. He was white, and so deep were his prejudices that he prayed to God that He would not put him in a room with a black man. God answered his prayer: he wound up in a room with *two* black men. The Southerner was furious and demanded to be moved out, but Reg said no, all his life he had been running away from his problems. When things didn't go the way he thought they should, he ran; he filled himself with alcohol and drugs; he copped out any way that he could. Now he was going to stay put and deal with his problem and walk through it in Christ. Within two months the Southerner became the best of friends with his two black roommates.

"Not all prejudice is necessarily bad," concluded Ken. "It is wisdom to be prejudiced about things that never change." Fire always burns, and a wise man doesn't put his hand in it. And God is always God. But products *could* change—a make of car, a brand of gas. And man was the most changeable product of all. "If we prejudge a person, we are saying that Christ cannot change him, and that is the greatest foolishness of all. He changed you, didn't He? You wouldn't want a person to judge you now, by who you used to be before you knew Him, would you? Keep in mind how easily your own point of view can be deceived or be just plain wrong, and it will help you in your dealing with people.

The buzzer sounded. If this class had been a sample of what the students were learning at the Farm, they were indeed getting an education."

7

"WELL, I'M TRUSTING THE LORD . . ."

Wednesday morning dawned cold and clear. Ken had an all-staff meeting at eight-thirty and had gone on ahead. By the time I caught up with him, the next thing on his agenda was a meeting with the staff of the farm, which also came under the Vocational heading. I asked if I might come along, and he said sure, leaning across the seat of his car and opening the door for me.

As we headed down the eastern slope of the mountain, I got my first close look at the farm. With its two huge silos side by side, its enormous curved-roof barn and freshly painted outbuildings, and its herd of Holsteins out taking the morning sun, it looked like it came right out of a national dairy calendar. And it had a feeling of "rightness" about it that I couldn't define; I sensed that somehow the farm was the anchor or cornerstone of the Teen Challenge Training Center at Rehrersburg.

Ken parked in the pleasant turnaround by the farmhouse, and we walked into the tiny office at the north end of the barn, which also passed as a changing room and a place to store things that didn't go anywhere else. Standing inside were four guys in wool shirts, coveralls, rubber boots and work jackets, and as it was too crowded to hold the meeting there, we reconvened around the big table in the kitchen of the farmhouse. Besides us, at the table were Hank Garling, the farm manager; Gordon Hameloth, the assistant farm manager; Tom Ferguson, a younger staff member who had requested the farm as his assignment, and a seventeen-year-old named Steve who had recently joined the staff specifically to work on the farm.

After opening with prayer, they got down to the business of the farm—rearranging the work schedule, discussing the week's milk yield and how the cold snap had affected it, and their real need for their #2 tractor to be fixed in a hurry (it had been in the auto shop for several days). Ken said that he would look into it, and then they got down to the most serious problem: the attitude of the morning milk shift. It had been deteriorating for several days, till, as Ken knew, the morning of the day before, none of them had shown up for their three-hour shift (which was the only work they were required to do during the day). As a result, two of the staff who weren't on duty got three hours of sleep that night. It turned out that one of the students had been sick and had an excuse, but the other two were written up and would find themselves on discipline, working every weekend, with all privileges lifted.

After that, Tom confessed that he had forgotten to see to the scraping out of the manure Sunday morning. The New Year's weekend had been a busy one for all of them, and Tom's mind had gotten onto his Sunday school class rather than on his other responsibilities. Hank had already spoken to him about it, but he wanted to bring it into the light in front of the others.

Finally, Ken asked them for their projections for the week to come, and the meeting was over. On the way back up the mountain, I mentioned to Ken that it seemed to me a good idea to have the meetings at the farm, as the farm people might have a tendency to feel separated from what was going on up on the mountain. Ken nodded. "That's why we began the weekly meetings, and there's been a real change since then. There's a thinking adjustment in progress now, but it obviously still has a way to go. Because as important as the farm is, the center's program still has to come first. A good farmer—and Hank is the best—would naturally put the farm before all else. But God is doing more than farming here."

Was the farm paying its own way? Ken beamed at the question, and it was apparent that the farm's performance gave him great joy. "When Hank came in 1972, our two-day milk base (average production) was around 5,500 pounds. This year, we expect it to be around 7,000 pounds, and 1976 was the first year since the beginning that the farm has operated in the black. After paying all its expenses and salaries, it was even able to make a monthly contribution to the center. Not a lot, but every bit helps."

Were any of the other shops in the black? "Only one, the print shop. You have to remember that they're really training areas where the men work only three hours a day, and there's a constant turnover of workers. No sooner do you begin to get a man trained, than he graduates, and a new man who knows little or nothing takes his place." He got out of the car and looked over the buildings on the lower level. "Still, it's my dream that one day all the shops will be in the black."

Were any of the others close? How about the body shop? "The body shop is coming along, especially now that we have a man heading it who was in the business himself for ten years. But we can't charge the rates that a commercial shop would, because our men aren't skilled enough, or able to work that fast. The auto mechanics shop is primarily occupied in maintaining the Farm's vehicles. The greenhouse," and here he pointed at a quonset-shaped, plastic-coated structure that was roughly twenty by eighty feet, "has only been in operation for a year. Even so, it made over $1,000 last year growing flowers in the summer and tomatoes in the winter. Of course, if a local florist hadn't given us all our seed and supplies, we probably would have made only half that. It's not much, but it's a start."

Ken had told me about the building of the

greenhouse, the evening before. Once Reg had given the green light to the project, he had spent half a year scrounging the necessary pipe for the frame, and other equipment. The same local florist, to whom Ken had gone for some pointers, was instrumental in it all coming to pass, giving them pipe, a circulator motor, and even the plastic they would need to cover the structure, as well as free advice. The Vocational Division welded the pipe connections, and in the end the whole thing wound up costing $1,000, thanks largely to the help of the florist. I gathered that the florist was doing well himself, and I wondered if he knew God was blessing him because of his generosity to His children.

But there was one incident concerning the greenhouse about which Ken was less than pleased. Last summer, some of the guys were pushing a pickup truck backwards out of the auto mechanics shop and into a parking slot at the edge of the upper level. When they got to the slot, the man behind the wheel went to apply the brake. He hit the clutch instead. The truck began to roll slowly over the edge. The man behind the wheel hollered, but he also froze and never did get his foot on the brake pedal. Over the truck went and down the embankment, which fortunately was not as steep above the greenhouse as it was above the print shop.

The truck picked up speed, and the guy inside hollered his head off. But he was not half as scared as the man who was sitting inside the greenhouse, studying a seed catalog, some thirty feet away from the point of impending impact. Suddenly, a great wrenching crash shook the entire greenhouse, and he thought it was going to fall in on him.

Regarding the drop-off now as we headed for the dining hall, I said to Ken, "I don't want to be presumptuous, but has anyone ever thought of putting up a guardrail?"

"It's on our list," Ken said, and we went in to lunch.

There was one division head I still had to talk to, and that afternoon I went over to Public Services to see Bryan Rainbow. Located in the basement of the single staff quarters, Public Services consisted of a room with several desks in it, a tape duplicating room, and a small sound studio, just big enough for an engineer, an interviewer, and two interviewees. Inside the studio, the walls were covered with foot-square egg carton separators, which made very inexpensive and very effective sound baffles.

Bryan would be coming over in a few minutes, I was informed, and as I waited, I listened as the morning's tapings of five-minute radio programs were being edited. Consisting mainly of interviews by Reg Yake with various students in or near their final termination month, these broadcasts went out to a dozen participating radio stations in the East.

"Hey, man," called a tall, cool Puerto Rican staff member named Sammy, to someone just coming in the door, "you got company!"

This was Bryan—young, soft-spoken, of medium height, with a moustache and a puckish smile. He suggested that we talk in the studio, and the first question I asked him was about the name, Public Services. The first time I'd heard it, I'd vaguely thought of a utility company or janitorial service.

"The name is actually a combination of two things: Public Relations, and what we would call Christian Services, or the evangelistic outreach of the center—the choir tours, the missions to churches, the broadcasts, the jail ministry, the visitors' services in the chapel, and the talks to high schools and civic groups." Public Services was also responsible for the bimonthly newsletter that went out to some 30,000 people on the Farm's mailing list. That meant that the mail room came under them, as well as the bookstore and the maintenance of the center's audio-visual equipment.

The choir had some twenty-five students in it presently, and was under the direction of Priscilla Oliver. They had already cut two records (as had Bryan himself), and they were invited to sing in various churches as often as two and three times a week. Bryan, or one of the other staff members, would take several students to speak at different churches or schools, where they might show one of David Wilkerson's films, or the slide presentation of the Farm, and then give their testimonies. The call for such appearances fluctuated, but it averaged about seven times a week.

How did Bryan come to the Farm? "My dad

worked here for eight years, before he went back to pastoring, beginning when I was fourteen. And then, when I was in college, I used to come down and work here during the summers—"

"Your dad used to be on staff here?" I cut in.

"Yeah, he was the academic dean, and so I sort of grew up with the place. A year after I finished college, I joined the staff here, and that was two and a half years ago."

What were the meetings like that they went to? They would go to any church that invited them to present the message of Teen Challenge. This was their primary purpose, though they might counsel some people afterwards, if they came up and requested it. Young people seemed especially receptive to their message, and they found their best audiences in high schools and jails, rather than churches. In fact, on more than one occasion, they encountered mild skepticism in some churches.

"One lady came up to one of the guys who had just given his testimony, and said, 'You weren't *really* that bad, were you?' The guy came on a little strong in reply to that, saying, 'Lady, why on earth would I put you on about stuff like that?' That was my reaction, too, until I stopped to think what had prompted her question. You see, our guys look so cleaned up now—and they *are* cleaned up, inside, as well as out—that it's almost impossible to believe the way they were before. I almost wish we had some pictures of the guys, the day that they first came into an induction center. If these people could see the long, wild hair, the wasted bodies, the dead, staring eyes . . . if they could hear the mumbling, disconnected speech . . . if they just got one downwind whiff of them . . ." his voice trailed off.

When Teen Challenge did speak in high schools, they would often be instructed to do so without mentioning the name of Jesus Christ. That would appear to be quite a problem in the matter of giving testimonies, but the Holy Spirit was equal to it. Don Wilkerson liked to tell of the time that he took two fellows to such a meeting. The first got up to give his testimony and said, "I was a drug addict, until one day I met a Friend. And ever since I've known that Friend, my life has been different. I'm clean, a new person." And then the second guy got up to give his testimony: "I met the same Friend he just told you about. And meeting Him had a similar effect on my life." When the question-and-answer period came, the hands shot up: "Who was that friend?"

Not all of the questions were positive, though. Some of the things that Bryan and others were asked indicated how much the inquirers were unconsciously expressing their own rebellion. Girls would ask, "Why don't you have girls in the program? Are they allowed to stay out at night? Can they go home?" And guys would ask, "You mean, they've got to do whatever they're told, and that's it?"

Bryan would remind them that the program was voluntary, that "there are no fences on our property, no dogs; the fellows have 225 acres on which to walk, and they don't go around like monks with their heads bowed and hands pressed together in prayer, bumping into trees." If they seem mature enough, Bryan will suggest that they consider what goes on at co-ed colleges these days, and then ask them how long they thought the program would last under those conditions. "I ask them to imagine what would happen if just one of our fellows went into town and got drunk? How quickly would those who were down on Teen Challenge or Christianity jump on that?"

I asked Bryan to tell some more about the civic groups they spoke to. "Well, occasionally, we get what amounts to a call for help from a town which suddenly finds it has a real drug problem on its hands." It turned out that he had been to such a meeting the night before. A town in the Poconos suddenly had eight of its kids leave school because somebody had given them bad pills, and they'd all gotten sick.

It took two hours for Bryan and one other guy to get there, at which time they found that they had to face all sorts of barbed questions about Teen Challenge. Bryan prayed for patience and tried to show them why drugs probably came into their community, and the responsibility that they themselves had to take for it. And on behalf of the Farm, he agreed to come back for a four-day weekend mission, bringing a dozen guys with him to speak at all six of their schools, as well as hold a rally in their youth civic center on the last night.

In the end, he leveled with them. "I can

guarantee that we will have an impact on your young people, but we are not able to turn them upside down. You're going to have to face the fact that you cannot continue bringing in outside groups to do your work for you. *You* have to start being open and honest with these kids yourselves."

Then Bryan shared a few of his dreams, then, of expanding their radio coverage into the South, of developing a regional-type broadcast, or—

"How are you going to do all this?" I interjected. "Alone, by yourself?"

"Well, I'm trusting the Lord . . .," and we both laughed.

Bryan said that when he came, there were so many things that he could see that could be done or needed to be done, he said, "Lord, it seems like it will take a million years; we'll just have our foot in the door by the time you return." But looking back, it was really astonishing how much they'd been able to accomplish in a very short time. Which was, I remarked, a good indication of the heavenly assistance they were getting.

"You mean, like how we got the billboards?" Bryan said.

I hadn't meant the billboards, but I asked him to tell me about them. "With the amount of time Americans were spending behind the wheels of their cars these days, I learned that billboards were rapidly becoming the in-vogue advertising medium, especially along thoroughfares as heavily traveled as I-78.

"We were coming back from a camp near Harrisburg this past summer with a busload of guys, when just before our turnoff, I saw this empty billboard, with 'This space for rent' on it and a phone number. I'd seen that billboard before, but now I suddenly said to one of the other staff members, 'Paul, write that number down,' and I thought to myself, 'Lord, I'm going to trust you for that space.'"

Bryan called the number the next morning, and it turned out that the same outfit had another vacant billboard, just on the other side of the Rehrersburg turnoff, facing traffic coming the other way. Both billboards, for some reason, had been vacant for months. "You don't have to say it was the Lord," said Bryan, "but it was a pretty unusual coincidence to have them so ideally situated, and the agents unable to sell them."

At length, Bryan brought himself to ask the sixty-four-dollar question, and found that the answer was considerably more than sixty-four dollars. In fact, the rental was so high that Bryan told him sadly that the center couldn't possibly afford it. He thought that was the end of it, but the man then asked what the center could afford. Bryan reserved comment until he could talk to Reg, and that afternoon was told that he would have to raise the money separately for such a venture; there was no way that it could come out of the Farm's limited operating expenses. Bryan agreed, made his best deal (more than a third off of the original asking price), and then wrote to three friends of the Farm, stating the need and leaving the amount open.

In a week's time a check arrived in the mail that would cover the first four months' rental. Bryan felt close to tears; he and his wife Carol started praising God, and he ran up to Reg's office to share the news. Reg gave his approval then, with the remainder to be raised from part of the proceeds from the next annual walk-a-thon. And I agreed that the billboards made a very favorable impression on anyone seeing them for the first time, as I had, four days before.

"You know," said Bryan, thoughtfully, "up until about six months ago, I used to think I would stay here for three, maybe four years. But now I've gotten to the place where I no longer think that way, because there's so much that can be done and I want to grow with it."

I told Bryan that he was the third person I'd talked to, to say such a thing.

8

"YOU CAN'T FEIGN LOVE"

My next stop was the auto mechanics shop. I intended to see each of the vocational shops, and I started with this one for a personal reason. My car was getting very balky in starting, and I wanted to see about the possibility of getting a tune-up. The garage looked and smelled exactly like a thousand other garages, except that there was a pit, instead of a lift. Asking for the shop supervisor, I was told that Eddie Doolin was away, putting the finishing touches on a new duplex for married staff, of which his would be one of the families moving in. The man in charge would be John Buchanan.

Was he around? "You'll find him over yonder," I was told. Over yonder meant the other end of the three-bay garage, where a short young man with an old fatigue cap perched on the back of his modest Afro, was working on an old Ford tractor. As I came to him, I saw that in one hand he had a fistful of old wires, and with the other, he was very carefully separating out one at a time from the jumble and tracing it back to the source. I watched him without saying anything, as he slowly replaced the old wire with a new one.

"*Got* to be careful," he said, in reply to my unspoken question. "If I was to just take these old wires and yank them out of there like this," and he made as if to do so, "I'd never get the thing rewired. This way, it takes time, but we'll have it running in a day or so." He got to a stopping place, straightened up, and wiped his hands on his pants. "What can I do for you?"

I told him about the book, and he snorted. "Well, we fix cars here. And trucks. And occasionally, tractors." He looked at the old Ford with a mixture of affection and disgust. "You know, those farmers, they bring an ancient piece of machinery like that in here, and they think they know just what's the matter with it. But it's so old, it could be that, or it could be a whole mess of other things. So you got to check it all out."

I imagined that that kind of thoroughness paid off in the long run. "Yeah, it does. Can't be messing with old tractors all the whole time."

Did any of the guys who came to work there have previous experience? "Some have worked on cars before. Mostly their own. But with most of the guys who come here, we have to start from scratch."

Did they do much outside work? "Some." Would I be able to get my car tuned? "How long you here

95

for?" I told him. "See me tomorrow, around one o'clock. We may be able to take you then, or if not we'll get to it Friday." I thanked him, and seeing that I was keeping him from his work, I left.

It was getting dark when I went outside, and I glanced at my watch: almost four. What now? The thought came to me that the gym class ran from four to five, so I went down to the lower level and walked in the side door. I blinked: it was like stepping into another world—a bright world, with powerful flood lights far above and a breathtaking white tile floor, with a basketball court in blue tile. It made a stunning combination, and I wondered what ever became of the blond wood, highly varnished gym floors that I had grown up with. And the roof was so high above that you could easily play tennis inside.

Some twenty guys were shooting baskets at one end of the court, and I walked down the sidelines to talk to Al Rainbow, Bryan's brother, who was the staff member in charge. The Farm, I learned, had a basketball team, but it did not have a regular outside schedule. Instead, they played various church and unaffiliated teams, whatever Al and John Waddingham, the other staff member in charge, were able to set up. How did they usually do? It varied, because of the turnover in players, but they often came out ahead at the end of the winter.

Al excused himself then, and I realized that it was past four, and I'd cut into their hour. He called the students together for calisthenics, then had them count off by two's for a volleyball game. One of the guys asked me if I'd like to play. I said no and spent the rest of the hour wishing that I'd accepted.

But it was fun to watch. Without knowing which guys had been in the program the longest, it was possible to make an educated guess: they were the ones passing the ball forward and setting it up for someone else on their team to make the over-the-net shot. Whereas, the loudest guys, who were being "the superstars," were probably fairly new to the Farm. These were the ones who would boom the ball from the back of the court, and try for spectacular shots which had little chance of success. Yet all but a few were giving the game everything they had, even to diving flat out on the floor to make incredible saves.

On second thought, it was probably just as well that I was sitting on the sidelines.

That night, since Ken and Joyce Isom and their two daughters would be leaving for Oklahoma the following noon to show the new film for Teen Challenge and to see their families, we had a farewell banquet: build-your-own hamburgers, french fries, and ice cream sundaes. A lingering thought of dieting was happily put aside, and we spent the evening sharing as if we'd known one another for far longer than four days.

Thursday morning again dawned fair, but so cold that the thermometer I'd affixed to the dashboard of my car registered ten degrees. Shivering, I fished the car keys out of my pocket and wondered if there would be enough of a charge left in the old battery to turn the engine. As I turned the key in the ignition, there was a low, deep growl from beneath the hood, like a bear being disturbed in mid-hibernation. And then silence. I turned the key off, then turned it back again. There was nothing, not even a clicking, and I had visions of the oil gripping the crankshaft like tar.

Ken came out of the house then and started his car right up. He rolled his window down. "You're welcome to ride with me, or you can use the battery on the floor of the garage for a jump. But I'm going to have to leave now for the staff meeting." I carried some heavy-gauge copper jump cables in the trunk, so I thanked him and told him I would try the battery. It did the job—barely. Coughing and sputtering like it had a severe case of postnasal retard, the engine came to life. I drove off to the center, reminding myself that I had to do something about getting the battery charged.

Don't show the buildings, show the people. The first person I wanted to see was the person who had been with Teen Challenge the longest, Ruth Cowgill. Ruth was an older lady, who wore her gray-streaked hair up, so sweet and modest that at first one might wonder if she were not completely out of her element here. And when I asked her what she did at the center, it seemed to bear out that impression. "Well, I supervise the mail room, and play music for the services, and I teach a course on the Psalms."

But if anyone should know that you can't judge a book by its cover, I should. Further questioning brought out that before coming to the Farm she had been dean of women at the Brooklyn center from 1964 to 1966, and had been an associate pastor for three years after that. I asked her then about the early days in Brooklyn, when she had been working with David and Don—had she gotten into street ministry herself?

"Oh, my yes!" she said, surprised that I would even ask. And she went on to describe several instances which revealed that beneath that gentle exterior, there was a wealth of old-fashioned fortitude. One occurred the afternoon that she and two of the younger workers were looking for a young addict who had called in, but since disappeared. Coming down the stairs of a dilapidated tenement, tired and discouraged, Ruth prayed that they would not have to go back to the center without having "communicated Christ" to someone.

On the front stoop sat a woman and two men, and as Ruth came out, she asked if they had seen the young man they were looking for, a drug addict who needed help. The woman turned on her and said sarcastically, "Everyone on this street is an addict! So if you're hunting addicts, you can begin right here!"

Ruth did start there, talking to them about the Savior who loved them—communicating Christ. As she spoke, she noticed that tears were beginning to form in the woman's eyes. "You're not hopeless," Ruth said to her. "Jesus came specifically for you." The tears spilled over and ran down the woman's cheeks. The two men listened without speaking.

As Ruth continued, she saw that a gang was approaching up the street, and at the same time, another was coming from the opposite direction on the same side of the street—their side. As the groups reached the front of the stoop, Ruth fell silent.

A man detached himself from one of them, came up, and put his hand on Ruth's shoulder. "Don't stop," he said. "We heard what you were saying, and we need it."

"You mean, you'd like a little sermonette?" And she used the word with perfect sincerity.

The man nodded. So Ruth gave them the scripture, "He came unto his own, and his own received him not. But to as many as received him, to them he gave the power to become the sons of God" (John 1:12). Then she shared with them that regardless of where a person came from, when he gave his life to Christ, he did become a son of God. There were more tears, and six of them were ready to make such a commitment, then and there. When she felt it was time to leave, the woman to whom she had first spoken took her arm. "Please, please come back to this street again. And bring others. We really need what you have here."

I asked Ruth if she found it quieter at the Farm. "Well, in some ways, but the boys are here longer, so you can really get to know them. And they get to know you." She paused and looked around. We were sitting in the dining hall, and a couple of students were wiping down tables at the other end of the room, but no one was within earshot. "You know, you can't feign your love for them. If you really love them, they know it. And if you don't, they know that, too."

She nodded toward one of the fellows wiping tables. "Two weeks ago, that boy was going to drop out of the program. I knew something was wrong; I could see it in his eyes. So I asked him if he would like me to pray with him, and he said yes." She beamed. "He's going to finish now, and he's much happier."

Ruth's ministry may have quieted some, but it was certainly no less vital. As I folded my notebook, she said, "Like I told my relatives when they asked me why I stayed here: I'm content. I guess I'll live and die here."

Driving the long way around to the dairy farm, rather than attempt the direct but icy route down the east slope of the mountain, I noticed an historic marker and pulled over. Once an Indian trail called the Tulpehocken Path had crossed the road at this point, and over it had passed the chiefs of the Six Nations, carrying words of wampum to Brother Onas (William Penn) in Philadelphia. Looking up the hill to the right, and to the stand of trees which crowned it, I tried to imagine a file of Indians in buckskin emerging from them and making their way silently down the hill. What a rich history had ebbed and flowed through the Tulpehocken Valley!

It was after ten, and I reminded myself how much there was to do. Pulling back on the road, I wondered which of the farm staff would be on duty when I got there. As it turned out, it was Gordon Hameloth, the assistant farm manager, a big, husky dairy farmer from Wisconsin. When I came in the office, he was studying a large wooden wheel on the wall behind a plastic screen. The wheel had different colored pins with numbers on them sticking in its outside edge all the way around. I then learned that each pin was a cow, and each notch the wheel could turn represented one day. As the wheel turned, the pins moved through the different phases of a cow's natural cycle. In this way, the farmer could keep track of exactly where every cow in the herd was—when she was ready for breeding, how soon she would calve, how long her maximum milk production would last, and when she would start drying up.

I was speechless. I'd never really thought about it, but I must have had some vague notion that nature more or less took its course, and the farmer's intuition more or less told him what needed to be done when. "Oh, it's not so much," Gordon said, when I marveled at the ingenuity of the wheel, which was sold by a food company. "Did the same thing myself back in Wisconsin with a wheel cut out of cardboard, some clothes pins, and some paper clips."

He showed me how they kept individual records on each cow, from which they could tell who her parents were and exactly how much milk and butterfat she was giving. The purpose, of course, for keeping such a detailed record was what Gordon called the "vertical integration" of the herd, by culling out the low producers, and by keeping only the calves of the best producers. With land and feed prices what they were these days, dairy farmers all across the country were being forced to think vertically, rather than expanding their herds.

In any event, vertically was the only way the farm *could* go at the moment, because the maximum capacity of the barn was 100 head, and the herd was at 106 right now. Each year some 100 calves would be born, approximately half of which would be bulls and sold off for twenty-five or thirty dollars. Of the remaining calves, the most promising would be held in the heifer barn until they were ready to be bred, after which they would be introduced into the herd, and the old and sickly cows would be weeded out. The average age of the herd was five years, and the ninety-four milkers were averaging forty-seven pounds of milk per day, or a shade over 5½ gallons. This, I was given to understand, was significantly above the national average for Holsteins, as was their 3.9 percent butterfat average.

We went into the milk parlor, and there, set off by

itself, was a gleaming stainless steel tank. It had a capacity of 8,600 pounds, and it was Grade "A" milk, emptied every other day into a milk truck sent by the milk plant of the local cooperative dairy. The milk went automatically from the milkers into the tank, where it was kept under deep refrigeration until it was shipped, to prevent any bacterial growth. "We'd like to flood that tank one time," said Gordon, "just to say that-we've done it. Came close a couple of weeks ago—8,500 pounds. But that was before the cold spell. We'll make her some day, though." I remembered hearing the day before that the average yield five years ago had been 5,500 pounds.

"Here's where the milking takes place," he said, walking around a corner and into the milking parlor, a long room, wide enough for six stalls on either side, and a lower level that ran down the middle. On this level, the milking crew could move up and down the line, cleaning udders, and attaching the suspended milkers, with their systems of hoses dangling down. The room was immaculate, its white-tiled walls gleaming. At the front end of each stall was a yoke and a feed bin, with a string that delivered exactly five pounds of special feed at each pull.

Gordon showed me how the cows came in, filing down a narrow, one-way corridor and into their stalls, and then back into the barn. And from there he took me to another side room, where a complex system of conveyors mixed grain, silage and alfalfa on a main conveyor belt. This belt moved up and down the length of the barn, distributing the mixture along the central feeding table. I had never dreamed how highly scientific and precise modern farming had become! And I had a nice feeling about it—it was good stewardship of what God had provided.

The main interior of the barn was a vast half-cylinder which reminded me of a blimp hangar. The cows were free to come and go as they pleased, and on a sunny day like this one, they were all outside in their fenced-in yard. The floor of the barn was all cement, which made scraping out the manure a relatively simple process. But with the old Ford getting rewired, they had to use the larger tractor which could not get all of it, leaving the remainder to be scraped by hand.

We climbed up into the hayloft at the north end of the barn, and I was pleased to see a mother cat teaching some kittens how to prowl for mice. Not everything had changed, I thought. Gordon walked to the edge of the platform and demonstrated how they forked hay down into the feeders. At the sound of some hay going down, a few cows still in the barn lifted their heads and looked up at us, to see if it was really feeding time. Gordon chuckled. "Standing up here and seeing all those faces down there looking up here and waiting to be fed, sometimes it moves the preacher in the guys, and they'll give a little sermon to the cows."

"Oh, come on," I grinned, suspecting that I was

105

being had.

"No, it's true," he insisted, without smiling now, and I believed him. In fact, I almost wished that there were a lot of cows down there, so that I might try it myself, but there were less than half a dozen cows within earshot. Oh, well, some Sundays were like that.

Did the cows have individual personalities? With so many, I was told, they tended to become impersonal. "Still, you do get some that stick out. There's one—I forget her number, but let's call her #17—who is mean to new students on the milk shift, or to anyone whom she senses isn't paying attention. She'll kick his hand as he's attaching the milker. We had one new fellow whom she'd done it to several times, and finally he blew up. He started really hollering about how #17 was tribulating him, and how she wasn't going to get away with it, because he had her on his list, and he was going to even things up with her." Gordon laughed. "We told him to calm down and next time, watch her foot and move his hand out of the way."

He pointed to a pail of purple antiseptic with a paint brush sticking in it. "Even so, just before Christmas, someone took that brush and painted 'Mary Christmas' on the side of her. And the word was passed among the new guys— watch out for Mary Christmas."

On the other hand, there was #88. Gordon did remember her number, as did everyone else who worked on the farm. A little smaller than the other cows, she was nonetheless a good producer, and unquestionably the friendliest cow you ever saw, a natural if Walt Disney ever made a cow movie. If you were standing in the barn, she would come up behind you and sort of nudge you in the rear, to let you know that she was there and wanted to be petted. And then she would follow you around, wherever you went. There was no question that #88 was the milk crew's darling.

Did the guys who liked working on the farm come from rural backgrounds? Some did, but most came from the cities. "I'll never forget one young kid from Brooklyn who had never seen a cow before. It was his first morning on the shift, and when he came into the milking parlor, he froze. There were huge brown animals everywhere, and he was terrified." Gordon smiled at the memory. "Well, we told him to get himself down into the pit and start attaching the milkers, like the others were doing, but he said 'No way!' I told him he didn't have any choice, and finally, he put his arm over his eyes, stuck his finger out in front of him, and cried, 'Pray for me, brothers, I'm about to touch a cow!' " I roared with laughter. "And then he said, 'Hey! She's *warm*!' "

When I got my breath, I thanked Gordon for the tour, and got into my car. As the heater began to work, a distinct aroma filled the car, and I belatedly realized that cleated boots were not the best footgear to wear around a dairy barn.

9

AMAZING GRACE

Wappita-wappita-wappita—the din in the print shop was incessant, and I wondered if this was another of those things that you got used to and ceased to notice. A photo-offset press was a fascinating thing to watch, regardless of the noise it made. Little metal fingers nervously adjusted the stack of waiting paper, keeping it straight and well-positioned, as a row of suction tubes came down on the leading edge of the top sheet, lifting it, moving it in slightly, and dropping it. The edge just caught the fast-moving belt that whisked it toward the printing drum, while other metal fingers moved in from either side and nudged it this way and that, squaring it up for the drum. In an instant, it shot out the other side and was carried along another belt to where it was stacked with the aid of still more metal fingers.

From the rhythm of the press, I guessed that the

process was repeating itself more than a hundred times a minute, and the speed could be adjusted higher. Under perfect conditions, it should be able to run unattended from beginning to end, but that was like saying that, perfectly executed, every football play should go for a touchdown. It was true, but it rarely worked out that way. In actuality, human fingers would periodically have to go in and straighten out what metal fingers could not cope with. A button would be pushed, the press would come to a sudden halt, and an unnatural silence would jar the ear, reminding the listener that he had grown accustomed to the din.

I looked up and saw that the supervisor of the print shop was showing some new students how to develop a photo-offset plate. When he finished, he turned the students back to his assistant, and came over to introduce himself. This was Aurelio Santiago, a black-maned, powerful-looking Puerto Rican, who had once gone through the program himself. When I told him my purpose for being there, he was happy to show me around.

We started with the jewel of the print shop, a 1908 letterpress, with a great iron-spoked flywheel, and a circular printing surface that flipped over like a flapjack. It was the first press that they had been given, and it had come complete with a chest of thin type-drawers. Aurelio opened one, to reveal a maze of tiny compartments, each filled with letters of type. They were filed alphabetically, except for the J and the U which came at the end, because they had come into use in printing later than the rest. That was how long hand-set presses had been in operation, and how little the system had changed. "No reason to change it," I could imagine a flinty old printer saying.

Looking at the ancient relic, so much simpler in operation than the highspeed Harris press I had been watching, and yet still ingenious in its solutions to the various problems printing posed, I could almost picture some inventor, working in a tool shed by lantern light, patiently tinkering with plates and rollers. Still, the whole thing looked like an exhibit in the Smithsonian Institution. "Beautiful," I murmured. "It's almost too bad you can't really use it."

"But we *do* use it," objected Aurelio. "Almost every day. As a matter of fact, it does all our orders and calling cards. It's a lot slower, but it makes a better impression." And he showed me some crisp, clean samples of the press's recent work.

After that, he showed me the steps of photo-offset printing, and again I was struck by the ingenuity which kept equipment in serviceable condition that should have been junked long ago. The photoengraving camera, for instance, was vintage 1939, with electrician's tape patching the holes in its bellows, and an old vacuum cleaner providing the suction necessary to hold the negative in place.

There was a homemade, under-lighted layout desk, and a couple of ancient varitypers for justifying right-hand margins. There were the two small offset presses, one of which could handle the four-color work—barely—and there was a folding machine. All of the equipment in the shop had been donated or bought at a marginal price, and it was amazing to me that the print shop had the temerity to take outside orders, let alone that it was actually running in the black.

I told Aurelio that I wanted to hear in detail how he came to the Farm, and since we had to talk loudly to make ourselves heard, he got us each a cup of coffee and invited me into his office. When he shut the door behind us, I was once more startled by the sudden quiet. He sat at his desk, and I settled back on the old sofa to hear his story.

"My mother committed suicide when I was two years old," he began. "We lived in Puerto Rico, and my father had gone to the States, to Chicago, to get a job and make a home for us. But as the months passed and he didn't send for us, my mother, who was fifteen at the time, grew more and more depressed, and finally killed herself. I went to live with my grandmother, but she was an old woman and died when I was twelve. So then I had nowhere to go; who wanted a twelve-year-old brat? And I was a brat!"

Since there was no one else, Aurelio wound up going to Chicago to live with his father, whom he had never seen. His father had tried to be a father to him, but Aurelio had so much bitterness in his heart that he resented the attempts. "Because he had never been a father to me, and I also blamed him for my mother's suicide, I never gave him a chance."

In the early sixties, as Aurelio came into his middle teens, street gangs were still predominant, and in the vernacular of the street, he started "hanging out"—drinking wine and smoking marijuana. He could remember exactly when he first took heroin, because it was the afternoon of his fifteenth birthday. Within a year, he had achieved another first: his first jail term, for possession of narcotics. Aurelio made good use of the time that he was in jail, studying high school courses, but it seemed that as soon as he was released, despite his good intentions, he went back to the old routine.

Gradually, the prison terms grew longer, and during the longest (four years), he passed his high school equivalency exams. But things were more complicated now, because during one of the times he was on the outside, he had married a good Puerto Rican girl named Martha, and had taught her to be an addict, too. What was more, they had begun to raise a family and had two daughters, but there was never any question as to what came first in their lives. If necessary, the money set aside for the children's milk would go toward heroin, and it was necessary more than once. "Those were the worst times," Aurelio said, "fixing in front of the kids. 'Go get me a belt,' I would tell the oldest girl, and I'd tighten it around my arm to make my veins stand out for the injection."

But Aurelio's self-disgust was mounting, and the day finally came when he felt that he had to do something drastic to change his life. And suddenly the idea came to him: go to New York. It seemed like the perfect solution—a new environment where no one knew him, where the police weren't looking for him, and where he didn't owe anyone money. So, one morning, without telling Martha or anyone else, he just left.

"Man, that all had to be the Lord, because no sooner did I arrive in New York, then I realized that I had just made the dumbest move of my life! Here I was in New York, with no money, no job, no friends, and a big habit to support. What was I going to do? The thought came to me then that I could go to a place I'd heard about, called Teen Challenge. So I called them up, figuring I could at least spend the night there, and maybe I could even get the money out of them to go back to Chicago."

The Brooklyn center told him that they unfortunately had a waiting list, but for him to come on in anyway and they would talk to him. When he got there, a chapel service was in progress, and when Teen Challenge worshiped, they sang with total involvement. Looking around at all the guys so happy, Aurelio didn't know what to make of it. How could singing a few hymns turn them on so much? And then he saw something he couldn't believe: among them was a big Polish fellow whom he had grown up with in Chicago, and had just recently done time with in the penitentiary. Now he was in the Teen Challenge program in Brooklyn? It couldn't be!

But it was. And when the big Pole saw Aurelio, he came over to him, and it was like old home week! How had the Pole ever gotten there? And then he started telling Aurelio about Jesus Christ. "I tried to turn him off at first, but then I thought, 'Why am I doing that? Why don't I give myself a chance?'" And when they gave an altar call, Aurelio went forward. For the first time in his life, he got down on his knees and prayed. "Lord, if you're really up there, I want you to come into my life." And when he got up, he knew that somehow his life was changed.

In the meantime, his Polish friend begged the staff to make an exception and admit Aurelio to the program, and they did, as of May 1, 1971. Some addicts, when they give their lives to Christ, are miraculously spared the agonies of detoxification; more often, it seems, God would have them learn by the experience of walking through it with Him. Aurelio was to be one of the learners. In no way were the cramps and the nausea, the aching and the alternating hot flashes and chills, diminished.

But during the worst of his withdrawal, some of the other guys in the program came up to his room and asked him if they could pray for him. He waved them in, barely able to talk, and they knelt by his bed. When one of the guys looked up, Aurelio saw that he had tears in his eyes, and that affected him more than any other thing during the entire time. "Being a drug addict, you get used to so much

114

gaming, so much conning. But this wasn't gaming; those tears were for real." It was the love that he had seen in the faces of those who were praying for him that kept him in the program whenever he wanted to leave, which was often.

Four weeks passed before Aurelio felt strong enough in his new-found faith to write his wife, and tell her what had happened to him. And meanwhile, Martha was having a bad time of it. After her husband had apparently dropped off the face of the earth, she had no more source of heroin and had no choice but to go to a detox center and kick her habit. Now, her skin all yellow from severe hepatitis, she was in a hospital when his letter reached her. She couldn't believe it, which hurt him, but not as badly as it might have; after all, he could hardly believe it himself.

After three months in the induction center, Aurelio was ready to come to the Farm, and after two months here, he was ready for his first weekend pass. He used it to go to Chicago; if his wife, who was staying with their children at her parents, didn't believe his letters perhaps he could convince her in person. "But I didn't come on holier than thou, because I knew one thing: with family, it's not what you say to them, it's what you live."

When Aurelio got to Chicago, he found that his brother-in-law was also living in Martha's parents' home, and as soon as Aurelio came in, he said, "Hey, Aurelio! We got some wine! Come on, we'll have a party!" But Aurelio politely declined. Then Martha,

115

who had been watching him closely all the while, said, "Aurelio, would you light me up a cigarette?" He took one, put it in her mouth, and lit it for her.

The next morning, when they awoke, Aurelio did not deviate from what had become his normal routine. He knelt at the side of the bed, thanked the Lord for the new day, and committed it to Him. Martha said nothing, but she never took her eyes off him. "But since I was not pushing anything at her, she didn't have anything to fight against," Aurelio explained. It was amazing, I thought, how much grace was on him at that time.

Later in the day, some of his old friends, hearing from his brother-in-law that he was home, came by to see him. They were practically bouncing off the ceiling when they came in, and they invited him to join them.

"No, I don't get high anymore. I live a different life now. I've become a Christian."

"You've done *what*?" There was a pause. "Do you smoke?"

"No," Aurelio said, smiling.

"Do you drink?"

"No."

"Well, what *do* you do?"

"You know, you really don't need to do all those things," he said equably. But he sensed that they would not be able to hear him if he tried to tell them about Jesus, so he just let the matter rest. Amazing grace.

Before he had come to Chicago, Aurelio had been

counseling with Mel and Frank Reynolds. With their approval, he had written Martha to tell her that he hoped she might leave their two children with her parents and come with him to Pennsylvania when he returned, and she would be able to stay with a Christian family in the area.

All weekend long she had not said a word about what he'd suggested in his letter, and he had not dared to ask. Now, as he was getting ready to leave, she said, "All right, Aurelio, I'm going with you to Pennsylvania. But don't you ask me to stop smoking!"

Inside, he was bursting with joy, but he struggled to maintain a cool exterior. "They're your lungs," he said casually. "Do with them whatever you want."

Martha came, and the same thing got to her that had reached Aurelio—the no-strings-attached love of the Christians around her, those she was staying with and those at the Farm. The day her cigarettes ran out, she just stopped smoking, and then, not long after she came, she went to church with the family she was staying with. Though there was nothing unusual about the sermon, the preacher, or the delivery, by the end she was dissolved in tears and came forward to give her life to the Lord. The very next day, at another meeting, she received the baptism in the Holy Spirit.

Martha was a new creature in Christ, but her self-life and her old addict habit-pattern still had a strong grip on her. So when an opening came available at the Walter Hoving Home, and Aurelio still had six months to go in the Farm's program, she went into their program. The commitment was for a year, and more than once she called Aurelio and told him in tears how much she wanted to leave. Aurelio knew what that was like; when she was still in Chicago, everything in him had wanted to quit the program and go to her. After all, he was a Christian now, wasn't he? But in his heart, he knew that God wanted him to learn more of what He had brought him there to learn, and so reluctantly he had chosen God's will over his own.

So now, when she called, he was able to stand with Christ, and she told him, "I wanted you to agree with me. I wanted you to say, 'Okay, come,' but instead, you're persuading me to stick it out." And so she did, and while Aurelio waited for her to finish, he stayed on at the Farm as a trainee, assisting the head of the print shop.

Today, he is that head, and he and Martha and their three children live in a home of their own, in nearby Myerstown. Martha has a very good job in a local company, and in addition to his responsibilities at the Farm, Aurelio is vice-president of La Casa, a Latin-American center for helping Spanish-speaking people, located in Lebanon, a small city half an hour to the west. Amazing grace.

Behind every well-run department is a good secretary, and Mary Stuart is the secretary for the Academic and Counseling Divisions. Before Ken left, he urged me to talk to her. And so, later that Thursday afternoon, I found myself sitting across the desk from a shy, quiet-voiced woman in a blue dress, who wore her blonde hair gathered back. Mary had been a secretary at the University of Maryland before she came to the Farm, and I was intrigued to hear how God had brought her from "A to B."

Raised in a liberal church, Mary had long felt the need for something real in life, something that mattered. In the course of her search, she found the Lord at an Oral Roberts crusade, at which she was given copies of *Voice* magazine, the Full Gospel Business Men's monthly publication of charismatic testimony. Moved by what she read, she went with much anticipation to the Full Gospel Business Men's regional convention in Washington, in 1967. There, her eyes were further opened, and she entered a new dimension in her Christian walk.

But one thing at the convention did not have the slightest appeal for her: the prospect of listening to a speaker named David Wilkerson. She had never heard of him, but many people were recommending his book, *The Cross and the Switchblade,* and making a great fuss about him being the one speaker to be sure to hear. The more Mary heard, the more she was turned off. He wasn't a Full Gospel Business Man; just some outsider, promoting his own ministry. And judging from the lurid title he had chosen for his book, it was probably a pretty sensational one at that. So Mary made sure that she *didn't* hear him.

Before she left the convention, Mary stopped to make sure she had plenty of charismatic literature to take with her, and when the man who was selling it finished adding up her bill, he said, "When someone buys that much, we give them a free copy of this." And with a grin, he slapped a copy of *The Cross and the Switchblade* on the top of her pile.

Mary managed a "thank you," paid her bill and left. She had too much respect for books ever to throw one away, much as she would have liked to, but she was equally certain she would never read it. And when she got home, she tossed it aside and forgot about it.

Some weeks later, it was income tax time, and like most of us Mary felt that anything that would serve as a quasi-legitimate excuse for not doing it was more than welcome. Mary's wandering eye fell on Wilkerson's book—well, *anything* was better than doing income tax. She picked it up, intending only to leaf through a few pages—just enough to confirm her suspicions.

She turned idly to Nicky Cruz's testimony—and couldn't put the book down. Nicky's life was so ghastly, so horrible . . . that God could change anyone like he was . . . she knew that He *could*, of course, but the fact that He actually *had*—that really turned on the light for her.

It happened, not long afterwards, that there was a Teen Challenge meeting near her. She went, and there she learned of the Farm, and of their first Harvest Festival that they were having that fall, and

120

to which they urged all present to come. Mary did come, with a girl friend, driving 150 miles each way to spend one afternoon at the Farm.

The trip was worth every mile. In the chapel service, she heard singing like she had never heard before—more than a hundred male voices joined and blended in praise! The place fairly reverberated with the power of God. While they were at the Farm, Mary noticed a sign asking for women to volunteer to do ironing, mending, etc. But what could she do, down in Maryland? Why, she could type for them, the thought came to her, and mail it back and forth.

It was a most unusual arrangement, but it worked out beautifully. And the next summer, thinking that they must have a secretary who would be taking a vacation, Mary offered to take her own vacation at the same time and go to the Farm to help them out. It was a crazy idea; she felt sure they would decline. They wrote back immediately and gave her a date on which to appear.

When Mary arrived , their secretary had not gone on vacation; she had just quit. But Mary had no thought of changing jobs, let alone any notion of ever working there regularly; it was merely a bizarre coincidence. But as the week wore on, she began to have the most peculiar feeling—I belong here. It was so irrational, everything was happening so fast, and yet each day the feeling grew—*I belong here*.

Was it from God? There was only one more day before her vacation was up. She prayed, "Lord, if

121

you want me here, have them ask me."

On the last afternoon, Frank Reynolds, the director then, came into the little office and said to the part-time bookkeeper, "We've been trying to figure out if Mary would like to take a permanent vacation here."

Mary looked up and found him smiling at her. "Why don't you ask me?" she said, a little surprised at her boldness.

"Would you?"

"Yes, I would."

That was eight years ago, and Mary has enjoyed every year. Before, life for her had been a matter of just coping; now, being where she was supposed to be, she knew the peace of God.

10

BEFORE EVERYTHING ELSE,
THERE WERE THE FARMS

There was one more person on my list that Thursday afternoon—the boss of the General Help crew, Tony Foret. Tony, whose name received the French pronunciation, "For-*ay*," was just finishing teaching in the last class period of the day when I found him. With his black beard and steel-rimmed glasses, Tony bore a striking resemblance to ex-Beatle John Lennon, but there the resemblance stopped, for Tony was not self-centered and he was genuinely concerned about the needs of others. Like Aurelio, he, too, was a graduate of the Farm's program himself, and I was anxious to get his story. And so, at his invitation, we adjourned to the staff lounge.

Tony was born and raised in a little town near New Orleans, on the Gulf of Mexico, where his father was the skipper of an offshore workboat, but it was not there that he had gotten involved with drugs. That didn't happen until he was in the army, first in

Georgia, and then more heavily in Vietnam. It caught up with him there and cost him an undesirable discharge, but it wasn't until he wound up in the addicts' barracks on Treasure Island in San Francisco, that he became a hard-core user. There, surrounded by knowledgeable users and dealers from all over the world, "I got turned onto drugs that I never even knew existed!"

Once back in Louisiana, his entire life became geared to obtaining drugs and turning on. He was searching hard for a reality beyond what the natural world had to offer, and in LSD and the more exotic biological hallucinogens, he thought he had found the supernatural, interior experience that he craved. "In fact," said Tony, "it was the only 'spiritual' or supernatural experience I'd known, for though I'd been raised a Catholic, had been an altar boy for seven years, and had even gone to seminary for a year, there was never anything the least bit out of the natural for me."

Tony was soaring now, on strange, iridescent wings, gliding over multicolored, geometric, inner landscapes that no man had ever seen before, and like Icarus, climbing for the sun. But also like Icarus, his wings would eventually melt, and once again he would be a reluctant sojourner in reality—until he obtained the means for his next flight. Then he would burst the surly bonds of earth and rejoin the vacant-eyed ranks of what Reg called "the spacemen."

But being an astronaut of inner space was

expensive. Tony had been arrested four times, and the last time they had come to his house with a warrant. They found his stash—as they had expected to, for he had made the mistake of selling drugs to a narcotics agent. Suddenly, it looked like he was facing ten to fifteen years. "So I began to get serious about it and started looking for a way out."

Tony got to see a psychiatrist, who recommended that he go to the federal drug rehabilitation center in Lexington, but that institution was preparing to shut down because of the disappointing results that were being achieved. (According to Dr. Hess, their cure rate was two percent.)

In the meantime, his parents were doing everything they could think of on his behalf, including contacting a Baptist preacher, who came to see Tony and told him about a program he knew of—Teen Challenge. Tony agreed to go enter the program at the New Orleans center, and his father was able to raise his bail. "My only motive," Tony admitted, "was to try to get out of those charges. I figured that if I did well in their program, they would go to court with me and maybe get the charges against me dropped, or at least reduced. There were no two ways about it—I was gaming it all the way."

But something happened that Tony had not counted on—he got saved. "It was the people," he said, as if that explained everything. "They were too much like what I'd always thought people should be like, but I'd never met any that were like that. They intrigued me. I was sure that they couldn't be for real. They *had* to have some sort of ulterior motive."

But daily Tony was being exposed to the example of these selfless Christians, and to some things he had never known: why Jesus had died on the cross, and that he, Tony, was a sinner along with everyone else (he had always thought that "good people" weren't sinners). And then one day, he had a revelation. "It came as a light—*I* was a sinner! I had always thought of myself as one of the good guys. And now I saw that I wasn't a good guy; I was a bad guy. But by then enough of the Word had been put into me that I also saw who Jesus was, and that He came for the bad guys." He nodded. "That's when I received my salvation."

Tony arrived at the Farm in July of 1974, and when he graduated, they asked him to stay on as a staff trainee. He was a full staff member now—and he was also married. How did that happen?

In Rehrersburg, a girl named Sue had her own beauty shop, and was also into drugs. (In *Rehrersburg?* Then it really was true what David Wilkerson had prophesied, that no town in America would be safe. For if there was ever a four-corners that would appear to be immune from drugs, it was Rehrersburg.) But among Sue's customers were Ruth Cowgill and some of the other women from the Farm. Sue sensed the difference in them, and while she never openly questioned them about their faith, the Holy Spirit had begun His convicting work in her heart. The women from the Farm were also praying for her, and so, while they were delighted, they were hardly that surprised when she told them that she had invited the Lord into her heart.

Some time later, Sue came to work at the Farm, and it was then that Tony, a trainee now, made his move. He struck up conversations with her and finally asked her out. And got turned down flat. Tony prayed then, and asked the Lord to search his motives, for Sue was an attractive girl. He had thought his motives were right, but now he wanted God to make sure. He did more than that. "The Lord flat out told me that she was the one." (I was surprised at that, for in my experience, God rarely made such pronouncements where a potential mate was concerned. I even knew of a few very humorous instances where a person had been quite certain He had done so, to the subsequent astonishment of the other party in question. I waited to see what would happen.)

"I was really inspired by that assurance from the Lord," Tony went on, "and given a lot of confidence." So he asked her out again, and again she said no. He asked her a third time, and for the third time he was turned down cold. And now Tony's faith was going through a crisis. "I had some really hard times with that. I'd say to myself, if she's the one, how come she can't stand me? And if she's not the one, do I know the Lord?"

Two more icy turn-downs, and Tony gave up. Fortunately, there was a great deal that needed to be done at the center, and now he threw himself into his work. One day Sonny Oliver, a staff member in the Counseling Division, said to him, "Hey, man, you and I have been invited over to Sue and Priscilla's tomorrow evening." Priscilla Tate was the choir director, from Saratoga Springs, New York, and she shared a trailer with Sue in the Farm's staff quarters. Tony couldn't believe it—had she finally heard from the Lord, too?

All the next day long, Tony imagined how that quiet dinner would go, and finally in the early evening he ran into Sonny, who said, "Have you eaten yet?"

"What do you mean, eaten? Aren't we going over there for dinner?"

"No, man, they didn't invite us to eat; they invited us for fellowship."

"You've got to be kidding!" Tony exploded. "I've been trying to date her for seven months, and now you're telling me she's inviting me over for *fellowship?*"

But earlier that afternoon something else had happened that now caused Tony to be patient and trust the Lord. He had gotten a call from his steady girl friend of the old days, with whom he had broken when she wanted no part of Christianity. She was in Chicago now, and she wanted to come and visit him. He told her that it was over, and there was nothing there. But the eerie coincidence of the timing convinced him that *something* important was going to happen that night, no matter how things looked.

What Tony found out later was that Sue had wanted to really get involved with the work of the

Lord, and had not wanted to be encumbered with any personal relationships at that time. But his discernment had been correct about one thing—her first and continuing reaction to him could hardly have been more negative.

But his perseverance in the face of such a frosty rejection finally caused her to seek the Lord in the matter. "I know how *I* feel about Tony," she told Him, "but I don't want to go against your will. If he's really the one you've chosen for me, then you're going to have to show me, and change my heart about him."

All the next week, she had a desire to be with him, and even had a dream in which she had lost him—which was odd, because she had never really had him to lose. But the next day, she invited him over.

Three months later, in the early fall of 1976, she and Tony were married in a ceremony performed by Reg Yake. But occasionally Sue still asks Tony what he would have told his ex-girl friend on the phone, if she hadn't invited him over the day before.

It was dark out when I left the center, and I wondered what I would do that evening, the first that the Isoms would be gone. I was just about to get in my car, when Hank Garling, the dairy farm's manager, drove up and got out of his car. He came to pick up his wife Betty, who did the center's bookkeeping. "Hey, Hank," I called out, "I need to get together with you sometime. Will you be around the Farm tomorrow?"

"Nope. Going to the farm show in Harrisburg." Well, what about this evening, after dinner? "Tonight, I was going into town (meaning Lebanon) to get some things." He thought a moment. "But why don't you come to the house for supper?"

I was torn—a home-cooked farm meal. But for that very reason, my own motive was more than suspect. Had I maneuvered that invitation? "No," I said, "I think maybe we'd better try to get together Saturday. I've got a lot—"

"I mean it," said Hank, warming to the idea. He turned to his wife, who was just coming out the door. "Is it okay to have Dave here over for supper?"

With me standing right there, what could she say? I remembered the times I had done that to my own wife, and how she had not appreciated it. Now, all I wanted to do was join the last of the snow that was melting and running down the driveway.

"Goodness, yes!" said Betty. "We're having chicken, and I've thawed more than the two of us can possibly eat. Come at six," she said with a big smile, and I no longer felt like melting.

There was a little less than an hour until that time, so I went into town myself, to the farmer's market in Myerstown, to get some food for the coming week. I was glad to make the run; my battery was low and it would help to recharge it. I had a thought about getting some gas, but I ignored it; there would be plenty of time for that later, and besides I didn't want to be late to the Garlings.

As we sat down to the table that evening (the same table around which we'd had the Farm meeting), I was relieved to see that there really was more than two could eat—or three, for that matter. There was a large platter of fried chicken, separate bowls of carrots, beans and corn, a basket of hot rolls, and a variety of things to go on things. I had heard of sumptuous farm meals but had never eaten one; I was about to partake of a great American tradition.

It was all very good, even the vegetables, but there was one dish that intrigued me—a dark red jelly that was apparently to be eaten with the meat. As I had some, I noticed Betty watching me. "What do you think of that?" she asked.

"Mmmm," I said, with my mouth full, and added, "delicious!" as soon as it was empty. "But what *is* it? It tastes almost like—beets."

"That's because it's beet jelly," Betty exclaimed, delighted at my astonishment.

"Best thing that ever happened to beets," grinned Hank, who had not had a great deal to say, up to that point.

While Betty cleared away the dishes from the main course, I asked them how they had come to the Farm. And now Hank did most of the talking. They had farmed all their lives in upstate New York, and now that their children were all grown and moved away, they wondered if there weren't something more that they might be doing for the Lord. Perhaps they might even start a Christian farm for the Lord, somewhere new.

Yet everything seemed to indicate that they would be staying right where they were. For one thing, they were in partnership with an older man, and while things between them weren't going as well as they might, they didn't have the money to buy him out, and he had no desire to buy them out. (It was not hard to see why. Hank took a great deal of pride in his work, and was an extremely dedicated worker.) For another thing, the Garlings were prominent members of their local church and deeply involved in its activities, and Betty was branch supervisor of the bank she worked in.

But what the insurance companies call "an act of God" suddenly changed all that. Hank and Betty came home one afternoon to find all kinds of cars parked in front of their place, including fire engines. Their barn was in flames. They never did find out the cause, but the result was that suddenly Hank and Betty were free agents. They started looking for a new piece of property on which to begin again, but nothing seemed quite right. In the meantime, they had heard that Teen Challenge was looking for someone with farm experience to help with their dairy farm at Rehrersburg, and so Hank and Betty went down to look it over.

Hank's initial impression of the farm could not have been less favorable. He was used to a stanchion barn in which the cows were yoked and held pretty much in one place, with their feed in front of them, and a manure gutter behind. It was much cleaner and more efficient than the barn they had here, where the cows come and go as they pleased, when they weren't actually being milked. (But, I thought to myself, the stanchion barn also reduced the cows to little more than milk machines, spending their lives standing in one place. It might be messier here, but it was also more humane—the cows were free to be cows.)

Hank was shocked by the feet of many of the cows. Because they spent much of their time walking around on cement that was always wet, their hooves stayed soft and kept on growing, till they had spread out like great pads, almost the size of snowshoes. The cumulative impact of such things left Hank and Betty having to pray hard when they got home, just to remain open to the Lord's will for them.

Finally, the time came when they would have to make a decision and let Teen Challenge know, one way or the other. So, one night Hank prayed, "Lord, you're going to have to let me know what you want me to do. If you want me to go to Rehrersburg, then you're going to have to heal this pain in my chest (which had been bothering him ever since the fire). But if you want me to have a farm here, you're going to have to make one available by the end of the week, when I have to call them and let them know." The next morning, when he woke up, the pain was gone.

That night—it was a Wednesday in the late spring of '72, and there was a church service that night—Hank told the congregation that he and Betty were moving to Pennsylvania. It came as no surprise to Betty; she had sensed it from the moment he had filled out the application blank. But the congregation took it hard. "Everybody was crying," Betty said. "We'd been married in that church and raised our kids there. It was like our family," and she passed a plate of homemade pastries to go with the ice cream that she had just dished out.

"There goes my diet," I sighed, helping myself.

"You don't diet when you eat out, do you?" Betty asked.

I laughed. "That's always been my excuse! I wouldn't want to appear rude." And I took a bite of one that tasted as good as it looked.

I asked them then, after telling them what I'd already learned, if they could give me any really unusual stories of the Farm. "Well, there are so many," said Hank, "if you really sat down and thought about them. But one does come to mind—about the time we lost a calf in the barn. She was gone for two days, and we couldn't find a trace of her."

"This may be a stupid question," I said hesitantly, "but, um—how could you lose a calf in an enclosed barn and barnyard?"

"Exactly what we kept asking ourselves," Hank replied straight-faced. "But she was gone, and there was no two ways about it. Plumb disappeared."

He stopped to pour himself another cup of coffee—and, I suspected, to let the suspense build.

"Well, sir," he resumed, "at the far end of the barn there's grating that runs across the width of the barn just inside the doors. Under that grating is the manure pit, and what we do is we scrape all the manure down to the far end of the barn, lift that grating and scrape it into the pit. When the pit fills up, then we get the little loader-tractor down there and push her out to where we can load it on the spreader." He pursed his lips and nodded. "Pretty efficient system," he admitted.

That was all very interesting, I thought, but I didn't care *what* they did with their manure. What about that missing calf? "I'm coming to that," Hank drawled, picking up my unspoken question.

"Finally, after two days of looking and not finding her, one of the students, a great big fellow named Melvin, gave out a holler. 'She's down here in the manure pit!' And everybody took off for the far end of the barn to see." Hank stopped to take a sip of coffee and then sampled one of the pastries. "Real good," he said to his wife.

"Hank!" I burst out.

"Well, sir, she was completely buried. Had her head stuck up to breathe, but it was buried, too. All there was showing was two little holes in the manure at the tip of her nose. Which was why we hadn't been able to find her. Was only the grace of God that Melvin happened to spot her at all." He nodded and fell silent, but spoke again, just as I was about to. "What happened was that the cows had kicked the grating loose as they walked over it—that happens sometimes, and we just put it back—but while it was open, the calf had fallen down in there. Then one of the guys, seeing the grate out of place, had put it back, without noticing her down there."

I was suitably nonplussed. "How'd you get her out of there?" I managed.

"Why Melvin, he didn't think anything about it; he just jumped down in there and pulled her out, as easy as you please." Hank chuckled. "And you know, today that's a part of his testimony. He tells it and then says that that's the way Jesus reached down and rescued him like a lost calf, from the muck and mire of sin."

And then he told a story, which I'd heard at least a half dozen times already, as it had become something of a classic for the whole Farm. A few years before Hank came, a young fellow who had come in through the Chicago center, and who had grown up in the city, reported to the barn the first morning that he was assigned to work on the Farm. Everyone was in the milk parlor, getting it ready as the first dozen cows came down the chute and filed into their stalls. "Wash that cow and get her ready for milking," called out the staff member in charge to the new guy, gesturing in the direction of the first stall, and he busied himself with the second cow, while the other two students of the shift took the third and fourth. When the staff member had cleaned the udder of the second cow and attached the automatic milking machine, he looked up and noticed what the new guy was doing. Holding a wet rag in his hand like a washcloth, he had just finished washing the cow's face and was starting on her neck.

We talked about the adjustment the fellows had to make coming to the program—and it was an adjustment for the Garlings, too, to realize that the most important thing was not the farming, but what happened inside the guys when they came here. I thought it was terrific that a kid, just coming out of hell, had a real chance to get firmly grounded in Christ, and that a former ghetto loser could come here, and in addition to being exposed to everything else, learn something about animals and farming. I saw a little bit then of the greater significance of the Farm. Before everything else in America, there were the farms, and if everything else went—if our computer-dependent technology collapsed for want of fuel—there would still be the farms.

Something else struck me, too. Don had emphasized that the most important teaching of all occurred not in the classrooms, but in the day-by-day examples set by the various staff members. It seemed to me that the example of industriousness being set at the farm was one of the best they could get.

The cuckoo clock in the hall went off nine times. I had stayed longer than I should have. But as I got up to leave, Hank said that there was one more story that I ought to hear, and I sat back down.

Normal procedure with cows just starting into their dry cycle, was to shoot them full of antibiotics and turn them out in a yard separate from the milkers. But a few weeks back, a serious mistake had been made and six freshly treated cows had been milked one more time. According to government regulations, if the slightest trace of antibiotics shows up in any batch of milk, the entire tank which it came from had to be dumped. The contaminated milk had been part of the fourth and final milking; the farm's tank was now full and waiting to be picked up, which meant that $600 worth of milk had to go literally down the drain.

As soon as Hank heard what had happened, he knew he had no choice but to open the valve and let it all go. But as he was about to put his hand on the valve handle, he got a strong check in the spirit—wait. So instead, he called the field man at the dairy and told him what had happened, and they sent a man to collect a sample, to be analyzed back in their lab in Allentown, some fifty-five miles away. The phone rang at three that afternoon: there was no trace of antibiotics. The milk could be shipped!

But that was not the end of the story. The milk truck arrived just in time to empty the tank before the afternoon milking. Hank washed out the tank and turned on the refrigeration unit, noting that the sides of the tank were already beginning to frost up as he put the covers on. Milk was perhaps the fastest breeding ground of bacteria and had to be kept barely above freezing, to prevent any bacteria growth until it could be pasteurized.

The next morning, sometime after the morning milking, Hank happened to notice that the tank's agitator wasn't turning. Alarmed, he looked at the refrigeration unit's switch; it was in the off position.

He lifted one of the covers, and the smell of rotten milk filled the room. From that stench, the refrigeration unit had to have been left off all night. Checking with all the personnel on both shifts, Hank could find no one who remembered turning it off, and to this day Hank has no explanation of how it could have happened. In any event, he was again about to open the valve and drain the tank, when again he got a check. Swallowing his pride, he called the field man for the second day in a row, and explained to him what had happened. This time they had to contact a man in Lansdale, some two hours away, to come with his microscope and chemicals and run tests on the spot. The man arrived and ran his tests, then called the dairy. "I can't understand it," he said over the phone. "The milk smells rotten. It should be teeming with bacteria. But I can't find a trace in it."

Hank was jubilant. "Even as we had us a shouting hallelujah time around the barn, the head field man at the dairy was telling the other fellow over the phone, 'There's no sense in us going over there when they have a problem; they pray too much.' "

I thanked Hank and Betty for not letting me go until I heard that story.

11

THE VERY BEST

I did a lot of dreaming that night, the way one does
after a crammed-full day. I dreamed of cows, mostly,
and they were hardly the sort of dreams that stuck to
the ribs of one's memory. Quite the contrary, they
would disintegrate even before one consciously
tried to bring them into focus. But I did have one
dream that stuck with me; in fact, it woke me in the
middle of the night and left me wide-eyed and
unable to go back to sleep, until I had recalled it in
detail.

In the dream, I was driving down a valley and then
up a mountain. It was a dirt road, narrow and steep,
running up the side of the mountain, without the aid
of switchbacks. I was driving a sports car with the top
down and a floor-mounted gearshift, much like one I
used to own, and I was changing gears frequently
and driving hard up the mountain. Near the top,
there was a fairly level, open clearing and several

roads led out of it, but I was somehow convinced that only one, the worst one, led up over the top and down the other side. I started for that one, choosing to disregard a sign by the side of the road warning that it was extremely dangerous, and a voice told me, in no uncertain terms, *not* to go that way.

But I knew better. I considered myself an extremely good driver, and the car was responding well, despite the increasingly difficult terrain. Indeed, I felt I knew the car so well that it was like an extension of my own body. Together, we would handle any road, and if it did get too bad, I would be able to stop in time and, if necessary, back down. So, on I charged.

For a while, I was doing okay. The road was tortuous; it was little more than a path, actually, strewn with rocks and massive roots and every corner was a blind one. Nevertheless, red-lining the tach in first gear, I made it to the top and started down the other side. I was just beginning to pick up some speed, when suddenly the road dropped away beneath me, and I was sailing out into the air like I'd just come off a ski jump. I had plunged over the edge of the mountain, and glancing down, like a pilot over the side of his open cockpit, I could see little square fields and hedgerows in the valley far below. And then the car began to plummet earthward, and I woke up.

Once the dream had been recalled, however, I promptly put it out of mind and went back to sleep. It is doubtful that I would ever have thought of it again, were it not for what happened the following morning. For Friday, the 7th of January, marked the beginning of the "Great Winter of 1977." During the night the temperature had fallen more than forty degrees. Nor was that all that had fallen—half a foot of fresh snow was being blown into drifts by a twenty-mile-an-hour wind.

As I went outside, I had the distinct impression that I should leave the car where it was and walk the eight or ten minutes to the center. But to me, the snow was a challenge. And while I didn't have snow tires, I did have radials, and in my opinion, they were just as good. The thermometer on the dash said minus four degrees, and the engine didn't even grunt, when I turned the key.

By now I was cemented in the grip of my own willfulness. I got out the spare battery, hooked it up to my own for a jump start, and tried again. The engine turned over, barely, and coughed and sputtered, as if there were a blockage in the fuel line. Which, of course, there was. The severe drop in temperature had caused heavy condensation on the inside of the nearly empty gas tank, and now that moisture was icing up on the way to the carburetor.

But I would not quit, though with each try the spare battery got noticeably weaker. Finally, with its last gasp, the engine chugged and caught. As soon as I had unhooked the spare and put it away, I got in the car, and without waiting for it to warm up, backed down the driveway—or rather, slid, since the runoff of the day before was frozen solid under the new snow—and stalled. *Leave it*, the thought came, but I was adamant now, and begging a jump start from one of the few staff cars to pass by, I made my way to the Farm.

One look up that long, steep drive, and I decided that perhaps it would have been wisdom to leave the car home, after all. The mountain looked like one of those motorcycle hill climbs on a bad afternoon. A blue car, halfway up, was off the drive to the left and abandoned, trunk-deep in a drift. The car I had gotten the jump from was desperately clawing for a foothold on the ice and fishtailing backwards down the hill. Gingerly, I jockeyed around and crept back to Isoms'.

As I turned right, into the drive, I tried to get a little speed up to help get up the hill, and the next thing I knew I was in a spin, going completely off the drive and winding up in the ditch by the main road, pointing in the direction from which I'd just come. *Leave it for now and walk* . . . but no, the least I was going to do was leave it properly parked. By rocking the car backward and forward, I was able to work my way out of the ditch.

This time, I would come at the driveway from the other direction, to take advantage of the slight slope in the main road. I rolled to the bottom of the slope, then back up it, well past the Isoms', stopped and started forward. I had good momentum when I got to the driveway and cut the wheel to the left, coming as close to the newspaper box as I dared. Up I went, and then suddenly I was in a four-wheel drift slide sideways, way off the driveway and down a steep pitch into the ditch. "Jesus, help me!" I muttered, and I wondered if the car would roll over.

It nearly did. When it came to rest, I practically had to climb up the seat to get out. Standing there, looking at the car with its left rear wheel hanging in the air, I didn't even want to touch it, for fear it might be that precariously balanced. I turned and started walking towards the center, which I should have done an hour before. With each step, I grew more angry. How could I have been so bullheaded as to ignore all those warnings! If nothing else, that first trip into the ditch should have done it.

I asked God to forgive me for my willfulness, and I thanked Him for His grace which had kept the ending from being any worse. After that, I felt peace and wasn't even anxious about how I was going to get the car out. But I still sensed that there was something more that the Lord wanted me to see. It was then that I remembered the dream. That, too, had been a specific warning—that my extremely high opinion of my driving ability was about to put me in real peril. I saw then, that my own opinions and prejudice—the very thing that Ken had warned his class to beware of—had so blinded me that I could not have heard God, even if I'd wanted to, which was a very dangerous place to be. That was what He had wanted me to see, and I was grateful for the lesson, even if I'd had to learn it the hard way.

When I got to the top of the mountain, I looked for Tony Foret. If anyone would know what to do about my car, he would. I didn't have far to look. Tony was behind the wheel of a huge army truck equipped with a great plow that was bearing down on me, as it cleared the drift-clogged access routes. I leaped out of the way and cheerily waved, and Tony nodded in acknowledgment, without breaking his concentration. Extricating myself from the snowbank, I decided to wait inside and warm up until such time as there was a pause in Tony's operation.

Ken told me about the surplus army vehicles that I had seen here and there on the mountain. The Farm, as a nonprofit, charitable organization, was in line (albeit last in line) to purchase used military vehicles from the government. Some of their buys had been real windfalls, such as the $14,000 coach bus which had had its rear end burned out by a fire, and which the Farm had bought for $40. Once they found another engine to fit it, they figured it would only cost $1,000 to restore it. At the moment, however, it was not certain that the big truck would wind up in the windfall category; though it cost only $300, in heavy work it seemed to consume a quart of oil every fifteen minutes.

Occasionally, areas of the mountain would begin to resemble a junkyard as they waited, sometimes months, for key parts needed to restore their bargains. But in the long run, it was unquestionably worth it, and it went along with a growing impression I was forming of the Farm: of an extraordinary amount of resourcefulness and ingenuity making the most of a minimum of serviceable equipment. It reminded me of the old Coast Guard and its Navy hand-me-downs.

Outside, there was a sudden silence; the roar of the Army truck had ceased. I went out to see Tony, and found him standing on the hood of the big 6 by 6, waiting for more oil. When it came, he bent down and undid the hood latches, jumped off, and sending the same helper for more water, raised the hood. He poured the oil in, and added the water to the radiator, when it came, then motioned for silence. You could barely hear a soft dripping on the snow.

"Thing's leaking everything!" he said in disgust, slamming the hood down. Tiny puddles were already beginning to form under the truck. I waited discreetly, until he noticed me, and explained my problem, embarrassed to be adding to his list of concerns. "No problem," he said, with a smile that instantly assured me that somehow everything was going to be all right. "I'll take care of you, as soon as I finish here and get Mary Stuart dug out."

Relieved, I went back to the Isoms', to work there and await Tony's help. In a surprisingly short time, there was the sound of a truck, and there was Tony and one of his General Help crew, backing the center's four-wheel-drive pickup toward the rear of my car. He found a place to attach his chain to my car's frame and told me to get in to hold the front wheels straight. Carefully, he crept forward till the chain tautened and my car began to come out of the ditch. It was over in five minutes. I thanked Tony profusely as he left on other errands of mercy, and I headed for

146

the center. The sun had come out, and by this time the Farm's drive was so plowed and salted and sprinkled with ashes that it was probably the safest road in Tulpehocken County! I parked outside the auto mechanics garage and gladly left it there to await John Buchanan's convenience.

I had one more shop to check out, and then I wanted to spend the rest of the day and the day after, talking to different guys who were now in the program. When I opened the door to the body shop, I was assailed by the sound of electric sanders, and I walked into a haze of paint dust, peering around for Dick Godfrey, the shop supervisor. The shop enclosed a large area, and it was filled with a big bus, a paneled van with its windows masked with newspapers and tape, ready for spray painting, another army truck, and several private passenger cars.

I found Dick in his office, and was glad to catch him as I'd been by the day before and missed him while he was on a parts run. Dick was a round-faced, easy-talking fellow in his thirties, with a shock of dark hair coming down on his forehead from under his red knitted cap. He showed me around the shop with pride, pointing especially to the van. "I owned my own body shop for ten years before coming here," Dick said, "and in time what became the most profitable aspect of my business was cars that had been 'totaled,' fixing them up and selling them. Take that van over there. We bought that wreck for $150. We'll spend about $350 for parts and labor fixing it up for the center to use, and when we're done, it'll be worth around $1,500, which means a net savings of $1,000."

"Wait a minute!" I interrupted. "I thought that van already belonged to the center." Dick looked puzzled. "When I came in here looking for you yesterday," I went on, "one of the guys in the shop told me that it was Teen Challenge's van, and that seven guys from the Farm were in it on their way to a mission. The van rolled over and was totaled, but by the grace of God, not a single guy was even scratched!"

"Makes a nice story," Dick commented, when I had finished. "Too bad it isn't true." He looked at me, a twinkle in his eyes. "Sometimes the boys tend to get a mite over enthusiastic."

"I had a hunch I'd better check that one out with you," I replied.

At the time Dick came to the Farm, the previous March, there was no one with any extensive commercial experience in body work to run the shop, and consequently the caliber of work was not up to professional standards. And it was slow—some jobs had been in the shop for four months. But now the quality of the work had improved to the point where car dealers were sending their routine jobs to them, and they were turning the work out much faster—three days on most small jobs, five on a full paint jobs.

"How long do you think it will be before the body shop is in the black?" I asked.

"It's there now," Dick said. "I was hoping to get a chance to tell Ken before he left. Ever since the beginning of fall, we've been doing really good. And judging from the work we've got backlogged, and a couple of flat-bed trailers that I know of that will be coming in to be reconditioned, there's no way we're not going to be well in the black this year."

For ten years Dick had run a very successful body shop of his own, and when I asked, he admitted that it grossed between $50,000 and $60,000 a year. How had he happened to turn up in Rehrersburg, helping ex-addicts? "Well, I'd been born and raised in the Assemblies of God, and a couple of years after I'd started my own body shop in 1966, I got interested in drag racing. From that, it was dirt tracks and old stockers, and before long I was into late-model racing. By 1971, I was racing four late models of my own, and in my shop we did all the building and engine work. Then fire wiped me out completely, and I had to rebuild from scratch. I also started driving someone else's car out of Ohio, with the understanding that I would get thirty percent of the prize money I won. We ran in Ohio, Pennsylvania and New York, and were doing pretty well, but at the end of that year, for a lot of reasons, spiritual and family, I knew I had to give up racing for good. I did, and concentrated on building the body shop back up to where it was."

Something else happened in 1972, which may have influenced Dick's decision to get out of racing. He became increasingly afflicted with a disease that was not finally diagnosed until he entered the Cleveland Clinic two years later. He found that he had acute rheumatoid arthritis. Medication made it tolerable, and a year later the Lord saw fit to heal him completely. "For about two weeks after that you can bet I prayed really hard for the Lord to take over the direction of my life. What came to me was to call Teen Challenge. So I called the center in Erie, and they referred me to the Farm."

When he called, he spoke to Reg Yake, and not knowing what else to say, he simply said that he was a body repairman and the Lord had told him to call. "Well, praise the Lord!" exclaimed Reg. "Do you know that we have been praying for six months for Him to send us someone in your line of work?"

And how good of God, I thought, not to send second-raters or failures who couldn't make it on their own. He cared enough to send the very best.

12

"WHAT GOES AROUND, COMES AROUND"

For the rest of Friday and most of Saturday, I talked to a cross section of guys currently in the program—black, white, Puerto Rican and Mexican, some from major urban areas and some from smaller towns, some younger and some older. Each of their stories, was in its own way, unique and compelling; yet after awhile, a certain, almost predictable similarity began to emerge.

Whatever their widely varying backgrounds, each life was first given over to self-love, self-will, and rebellion, and then, after sin's season of pleasure, gradually consumed by misery, fear or despair. Whether the drugs or the alcohol or the emotional binges were initially an escape or a play for acceptance, they soon became master rather than servant. And a life which had once been given over to serving self, was in the end taken over by the cyclical bondage of addiction and criminality, from which there was no escape—until such time as God, in His infinite mercy, would put such a life in the path of resurrection, as via the Teen Challenge program, giving the individual an opportunity to choose the light and cleave to it. Such lives, once wrecked and totaled, were now in the on-going process of being renewed and reclaimed by Jesus Christ.

How to present these lives—I couldn't relate them all, and I knew God didn't want a composite. In the end, it seemed right to pick two, and the two that it seemed right to pick stood out not because they were outstanding, but because they were so typical.

Dean Booker was huge. At 6′ 3″ and 290 pounds, this young black looked like a slightly chubby defensive lineman, and one could imagine that he looked even more formidable a few years and some fifty pounds earlier, when his street career began. Despite a mother who was praying for him daily and a comfortable home in Harlem, Dean was in a hurry—for the flashy cars, the girls, the good times. At fifteen, he got a job as a bouncer in a restaurant bar on Manhattan's upper east side, and soon after that, as a bodyguard for a rock group.

From the beginning, the money was easy and came in almost faster than he could spend it. White people wanted heroin, but they didn't want to go to Harlem to get it. So Dean would go for them, and if it cost him $50, he would charge $100. He tried some heroin himself, just to see how it would go, and it

152

went fine. "I was making $200-$300 a day, and getting a good high, besides. But all this while, my mother, she's praying for me. And one day she lays the question on me, 'Dean, what are you going to do about your future?'

"Well, I'd never thought much about the future. I figured I'd save a few thousand and retire by the time I was thirty. Of course, I hadn't started to save anything, but there was no need, the money was coming in so fast. I'd have $200 and blow it, and I'd have another $200 before I missed it."

Sin's season of pleasure lasted about three years, and then it was over. The beginning of the end came when Dean's mother told him that she had a premonition that something was going to happen to him. Almost immediately, he was picked up for possession of narcotics. Since it was his first arrest, he was released with a warning, and was a lot more careful after that.

In the meantime, "I was getting really hooked on heroin. I thought I could control it, but after a while it got beyond me. And then my mother started writing notes and leaving them for me to find around the house, like: 'Jesus Christ can still change your life, Dean; He will deliver you from drug addiction.' Sometimes, she would put these notes in the pocket of my pants or tape them to the bathroom mirror. I would go into the bathroom to shoot up, and there would be this note, rebuking the devil. There was something about that note that would make me feel very uneasy inside, till it got to the point that I would have to leave the house to shoot up. And for the benefit of my friends who would turn on with me, she put a note on the front door, saying, 'Devil, do not ring this doorbell, in the name of Jesus.' It discouraged them, all right."

Now Dean started having prophetic dreams. Or rather, nightmares. The first was that he was in the back seat of a car, getting beat up, and a week later, he was in the back seat of a car, getting beat up. Next, he dreamed he was on the ground, and half a dozen guys were working him over. A week later, he was in the restaurant bar where he worked, and some guy said something to his girl. He thought the guy was alone and called him on it and got ready to hit him, when someone came up behind him, and hit him over the head with a ketchup bottle. Four or five more guys came out of nowhere and joined in, and the next thing he knew, he was down and they were hitting him.

Dean found out later that his mother had started praying that the Lord would give him specific visions of things to come in his life. It shook him badly, but it also convinced him that a supernatural God was at work in his life. So when his mother introduced him to a Christian FBI agent whom she knew, Dean agreed to go stay with him, while he kicked his habit.

"He took me to church one night, and when they had the altar call, I went forward. I knew he was hoping I would, and I figured I'd just go up there and put on the act. But when I got up to that altar, God was there. I fell to my knees, and all I could say was,

'Help me, please. I'm tired.'

"No sooner were the words out of my mouth, than something seemed to lift off me, and I started to cry. I felt the peace settle over me then, and I knew that Christ had come into my life, because when I got up, all the pressures of the world were gone, and I was like a little child, lost."

Two days later, he went up to Connecticut, to see his girl, and he smoked marijuana—one joint wasn't going to make a difference—and when he got home, a friend came by, and he got high. His mother was heartbroken. He had told her right away what had happened, and she thought that her prayers for all those years had finally been answered.

Two more days passed, and his girl friend came down from Connecticut. She was so enthusiastic to Dean's mother about the change she had seen in him that the upshot was they all went down to the Americana Hotel, where there was a Christian meeting that night. One of the principal speakers was a well-known Teen Challenge graduate, who afterwards prayed over Dean, telling him that he would be a preacher one day, and giving him the address of the center in Hartford. Dean's mother urged him to go, and he agreed. "I'm tired," he told her. "I'm going to do my best to get myself together."

And he did. At the time the speaker had told him he would become a preacher, Dean had thought he was crazy. He doesn't think so now; in fact, he can't wait to go to Bible school when he graduates from the Farm at the end of March. How did he feel about the program, especially the discipline? He thought a moment before replying. "I see the staff as men of God. Sure, they give us trials and tribulations sometimes. But I think God tells them when to give us the trials, because they always seem to know just when to bring it on you. I look on them as my family in Christ. . . ."

Frank Gutierrez was a quiet, heavily muscled Mexican, who looked at least ten years older than his age of twenty-four. With his metal-rimmed glasses which were tinted slightly gray, and his unwasted words and movements, it was not difficult to imagine the air of menace which surrounded him in the old days.

Frank came from the north side of Saginaw, which was the worst side. "I guess you could say that I was following the image—looking up to the people who had money. I knew they'd gotten the money the wrong way, and I figured that way was good enough for me, too. I started off young—I was about eleven, the first time I sniffed glue. Of my family, only my older brother cared what happened to me. He didn't want me out on the streets, like him, and so, whenever he caught me there, he would push me home. I see that as love now, but at the time I resented his treating me like a little kid. One time, he and his friends had a clubhouse in our backyard, and they wouldn't let me come in, so one day I just burned it down.

"I did gangs for a while, and then I really got into the faster walk of life—moving with women, drinking a lot. I was so young, I became a baby alcoholic. From there I started doing pills and grass and finally heroin. The first time I did heroin, I put it right in my vein."

Frank had no trouble supporting his habit. He had become a pusher, and the people he was working for paid him well. By the time he was nineteen, he had other guys pushing for him, and a job at Chevrolet, as a cover. But that job could never have begun to pay for the house he now owned, or the Cadillac and Volkswagen, or his wife's new car. Frank had made it, faster than anyone he knew.

"But there's an old saying in the faster walk of life—what goes around, comes around." And now it started coming around for Frank. "When I first started taking drugs, I did it for the highness, to be cool around the people. But now drugs had begun to take control of me. Now, I had to do what *they* said, instead of the other way around. Now, I wasn't taking them to get high anymore; I took them to keep the withdrawal sickness off of me."

And Frank started to lose his edge. For three years he had not been arrested. Back when he was seventeen, he had been picked up for attempt to commit murder, but he had "copped out on a CCW" (carrying a concealed weapon). Now, he began to make mistakes, and the police, who had him under surveillance, started picking him up. And at a time when he needed his wits about him more than ever, he began to lose his cool. Angry and suspicious, he began beating up on the guys who worked for him, with the result that they all quit him. That left him with no way to fulfill the quotas of the people *he* was working for, and so he had to leave and go into hiding.

About that time, his wife died behind the wheel of the car he had given her. After that, Frank stopped caring, and his situation deteriorated as rapidly as it had once improved. "I lost everything. I was no longer *the man*; I was just Frank. I used to dress real fancy; now I looked like a bum. And I was having a hard time supporting my habit. It used to be a guy would come to me for a fix, and if he was two dollars short, I wouldn't give it to him. I tried to be that cold-hearted type of guy—they had to come up with the full amount, or no stuff. But what goes around, comes around. Now I was out on the street, a couple of dollars short and begging the pushers to let me have it anyway, and they wouldn't have mercy on me.

"I had to hustle to get the money for my habit, and I went a little crazy, beating too many people, ripping off my own people, anyone." Frank was widely feared, and people found reasons not to be around when he started coming their way. But there was one guy that Frank was afraid of, a guy who had grown up on his street, named Salvador Flores. Salvador had not been around for a year, and Frank thought he must have been dead or in jail. And then one day, Salvador showed up.

Frank spotted him down the street, getting out of a Volkswagen with a white guy, and the first thing he thought was that they were going to set someone up and make an arrest. But there was something different about Salvador; he was no longer wild-eyed and long-haired. He was clean-cut now, and there was a sort of shine to him.

Frank stayed out of sight, but his curiosity kept him from leaving entirely. The two men—and that was one of the few times Frank had ever seen a white person on their block—were working their way up the street, talking to people and passing out things. Before Frank realized it, they had gotten too close, and Salvador had spotted him. He called out to Frank, and though Frank would have liked to fade away, because the last time Salvador had seen him, he was riding in some mighty big cars, it was too late.

"Frank," Salvador asked him straight off, "how long do you think you can continue this life?" And then Frank saw what it was that he was carrying under his arm—a Bible. So *that* was it! And Frank put up his tough front.

Salvador reminded Frank that he himself had been on the street before the Lord had come into his life, and he told Frank about the Teen Challenge program that he had gone through. Frank wanted to listen, but other people were standing around now, and he had an image to protect. So he stayed tough, and Salvador finally left.

"Things got worse, after that. I'd go back to the

159

place of the girl I was living with and try to shoot up, but I couldn't find any place to put the needle. I'd be all covered with blood, and in frustration I'd just stick it anywhere. One time, I was so nervous, I knocked the stuff on the floor, right out of the cooker. But I was hooked so bad, I went right to the floor with the syringe and drew it up off the floor. That's when it really began to dawn on me how far I'd fallen. And it was confirmed when my brother, who was fooling around with drugs, too, said, 'Look at you! Get away from me, *junkie!*' "

All during this period, there was a lady social worker who used to come to read the Bible to Frank's invalid grandmother and talk to her about the Lord. One day, she talked to Frank about Him, too, and Frank decided then to do the thing he feared the most—give up drugs. He had had to go off, "cold turkey," on the two occasions that he had gone into jail, and it had been such hell that he had promised himself he would never go through that agony again. But now, he had no violent reaction whatever. "All I had was diarrhea, which I figured was to clean me out. You know how a dead man has a smell, and that smell is so horrible, it makes you want to vomit? Well, an addict has a smell, too, and when he's kicking, and all that sweat and stuff is coming out of him, that smell is strong and all over his body. That smell covered me, but inside I was feeling nothing—no aching, no cramps, no nausea, nothing."

The social worker took him to see a pastor friend of

hers, who prayed with him, and Frank accepted the Lord. He told the pastor that he didn't feel any different, and he wondered if it was really going to make a difference, but the pastor said, "Just wait. The Lord's going to start sending so much your way that you're going to say, 'Wait a minute! Slow down! I can't take all of this!' "

The first thing that happened was that Frank began to be convicted that the Lord didn't want him living in adultery anymore, and by way of confirmation, He sent Salvador, who had been away in Bible school for a year, to see Frank. Salvador gave him a ride one day and said, "You stay with that young lady back there, don't you?"

"Yeah." Frank had no money, no place to go.

"You know that's not right, don't you?"

"Yeah." That was what Frank liked about Salvador; he always put it right on the line, whether Frank wanted to accept it or not.

"Well, what do you want to do?"

Salvador, I want to learn more about the Bible," Frank said, a little surprised at his answer.

"Then Teen Challenge will help you out."

But that was one place Frank did not want to go. He knew that he would have to submit to their authority, and that was something he had never done with anyone. And he was not about to start. But one afternoon, not long after their talk, he was alone in the girl's apartment, and so miserable that he started crying. Finally, he said aloud, "Lord, you know how much I don't want to go to Teen

Challenge. But if that's your will for me, then you'll have to go with me, each step of the way." And the next thing he knew, he was packing.

The director of the Saginaw center was Ben Stowell, and when Frank introduced himself, he told Ben, "I've kicked drugs, I don't smoke anymore, and I don't run the streets anymore. The only thing I want to do is learn more about the Bible."

Ben gave him a look of surprise and then put an arm around him. "You're the first person that's ever come in here because they wanted to learn more about the Bible."

"I don't have to stay here," Frank added hastily. "I'll stay with my mother, and come in when you have classes, and that will work out just—"

But Ben was shaking his head. "If you come at all, you'll live here, the whole time." And Frank knew that that was the right way.

It wasn't easy. The center was right in the heart of Saginaw's heaviest street temptations. But right across the street from the window of Frank's room was a funeral home, and it seemed like every day they had a funeral. Frank would look out his window at the people going in and coming out of that place, and it was a continual reminder of the fate that surely awaited him, if he left and went back to the streets.

When it was time for him to go to the Farm, and he was saying goodbye, Ben hugged him. "That really got to me, because no white man had ever done that to me before." And Frank started to break up at the recollection. "When I got outside, I was so happy, I just started giving out tracts to everyone I passed."

But the Lord had only begun to work on Frank's prejudice. "When I came to the Farm, my room was the only room with four different kinds of guys in it—white, black, Mexican and Puerto Rican. In prison, they always used to separate you, according to race. They did it so that prejudices wouldn't cause any more trouble than there already was, but what it did was feed the prejudice even more. So coming here, I never thought it would work. But we started learning from each other, and in Christ, we found that we could accept each other for what we were."

Frank would be graduating soon, and he intended to stay on for three more months, as a trainee. After that? Bible school for even more grounding in the Word, because it looked like the Lord might be calling him into the ministry.

One thing Frank said toward the end seemed to sum it all up: "That first week I was here, I was ready to leave every day. I would even sneak a shower when I wasn't supposed to, just because I didn't want anyone telling me what I could or couldn't do. I wanted to do things *my* way. But that isn't the way it works in the program," and he chuckled, "for which I'm grateful. Because now I want to do it God's way."

13

"JUST REMEMBER:
JESUS IS THE PROGRAM"

Near the end of my week at the Farm, there were two things that I regretted not having heard—the choir practice, and Reg Yake preach. The Lord, ever gracious, filled in both gaps later, and both on the same day.

I slipped into choir practice one afternoon, as the choir was in full song. Their director, Priscilla Oliver, with her hands was calling for more depth, and with her voice was calling out over the singing, "Words, words, words!" trying to get them to enunciate more clearly.

And they responded, giving it all they had, which was not surprising. I had learned that the choir was not necessarily comprised of the best voices in the program, but of guys who were prepared to give 100 percent. Their motivation *had* to be high, I thought, for them to gladly give up an hour of what little free time they had, every weekday afternoon, to practice.

But I also came to understand that singing in the choir was regarded as a great privilege. Because in many ways the choir was the most dramatic witness to what God was doing at the Farm. Choir members could expect to be called on at random for their testimonies during a performance, and all of them would fellowship afterwards with those who had invited them. Consequently, it was important that each member be spiritually on the ball, and any choir member whose grades went down or who went on discipline, would not be singing for very long.

The songs they were singing were mostly given by the Holy Spirit to various students in the past. And while some still had a catchy beat, or overtones of black soul music from the old days, the singers were totally involved. It was moving to hear, as much for the spirit with which the songs were being sung, as for the words and music themselves.

And that day I also got a sample of Reg Yake's preaching. He was disturbed about some attitudes on the part of too many students, and he let them know it in no uncertain terms. "It's great for you guys to come in here and sing the Gospel songs and have yourselves a fine old time. But how far do you take it outside this chapel? You sing, 'He's Lord of All,' and you walk down the hall and put down your brother. You take his socks, you cheat in classes, you don't show up to work on time. In here, you say, 'I'm a new creature; the Lord's done a work in me,' and you go out and play the same games you played on the street."

There was dead silence in the audience. "This Christian life is more than coming in here and seeing how loud you can shout and how high you can jump! This Christian life is *lived out*! You don't cut in line, you don't steal from the kitchen! And you'd better start living in Jesus Christ *now*! You'd better start living *for* Him now, and stop living for yourselves. Anyone can raise his hands in the air and praise the Lord, but it takes a *man* to stand up and start living for Christ! And what do you want to be, anyway, men or babies? Any baby can say, 'I don' wanna do this,' or 'I don' like the way they do that'—it takes a man to say 'no' to what *he* wants, and 'yes' to what Jesus wants!"

And now there was repentance—and enthusiasm. Muted expressions of, "Oh, yeah, preach it, Brother!" could be heard.

"You've got to *want* to be a new creature!" Reg went on. "You've got to want to badly enough! Sure it's a battle. But God didn't call you to be a bunch of pantywaists. This is a training center, and you're called here to be trained to be men! If you want to be treated like babies, why we'll pick you up and change your diaper and burp you. You want that? You want us to spoon-feed you pablum? Or do you want to be men? God's looking for soldiers, for men. He's not looking for a bunch of babies. So don't come crying down to the office, 'Poor little me.' You're in His army for keeps, man," Reg concluded. "You're a soldier of the cross!"

And now there were shouts of, "Amen! Amen! Preach it, hallelujah!"

Afterwards, Reg explained why the emphasis on maturing in Christ. "They get healed physically, usually before they come to the Farm. But the mental and emotional healing are much harder, and take much longer to accomplish. Part of the problem is that some of the guys have been on drugs for so long that they never had an adolescence, and now that they've been delivered from addiction, they start reliving what they never had. There are guys in the dorm twenty-seven years old, who are behaving like seventeen—horsing around with shaving cream, playing tricks, making up for all those years they missed. We tolerate it to a certain degree, but we don't have that much time, and so, after a while, we come in on them and say, 'Hey, man, you're not seventeen any more; you're twenty-seven! Your body is twenty-seven, and no one is going to accept you as seventeen. Least of all, the foreman; he's not hiring a seventeen-year-old; he's hiring a twenty-seven-year-old.' "

Reg frowned. "Another part of the problem is that once they get healed physically, they want to mentally put their feet up and take it easy. But the mental battle is the hardest one of all, because Satan's still hanging around just waiting to start working on them. So we keep a close watch on them, especially in chapel. A guy starts to fall asleep on me, and I'll call him out in front of everyone. He will be so embarrassed, he'll never fall asleep again. But it

167

has to be that way! Satan isn't wearing 16-ounce gloves; he fights bareknuckled."

Reg smiled. "You can almost predict where they're at by what month they're in. Sometimes, when the choir is away, I'll have two guys from each class get up and testify. The first-month guys will say, 'Oh, glory to God, am I ever glad that the Lord brought me to Teen Challenge! And oh, is it great to be on the mountain here!' In the third to fifth months, you'll hear the guys say, 'Boy, am I being tribulated! I almost wanted to split last week, but I'm hanging in there!' The seven-month guys are more subdued. They say, 'I almost split during my third month, but the Lord wouldn't let me go. And now I'm beginning to see why.' And the guys in their termination month say things like, 'What a privilege it is to go through this program! I'm ready to graduate, but I know now that God has only just begun His work in me. I've got so much more to learn.' "

But, in the meantime, Reg and the rest of the staff will have done all they could to prepare the student to reenter society as a fully functioning Christian. The closer he gets to graduation, the stronger the lessons become. Reg himself taught Church Relationships to those about to graduate. He would preface his remarks by saying, "The church is not perfect. There are going to be some people out there who are going to do some very cruel and hurtful things to you—and they'll do them in church, the one place you'd least expect them." And then he would pick three guys in the class and put three life situations to them, encouraging them to forget who he was and really put themselves into the situations.

To the first guy, he would say: "You're going to go to a local church. You're going to get happy in that church. You fall in love with a nice-looking chick, and everything is sailing along just great. And then her father finds out that you were in Teen Challenge.

" 'Teen Challenge? What is that?' he asks his daughter, and she tells him it's a drug program.

" '*What*? He was a drug addict? Well, you're not going with him!' And he searches you out and sticks his finger under your nose, and says, 'You dirty junkie, don't you come *near* my daughter, you hear me? I don't want you calling, I don't want you coming around my place, I don't want anything to do with you whatever!' Now how are you going to handle that?"

To the second guy, who might be black, Reg would say: "You've found an integrated church, and you're happy in it. You enjoy the preaching, and you're growing, really coming along very well. And some white guy comes up to you and quietly puts it to you—'Look, nigger, we don't want you in our church, so why don't you get lost!' What are you going to do?"

For the third situation, Reg would ask if any of them were married, and would address himself to that man. "Let's say your wife is going to church, and you join her church, and maybe even give your

169

testimony. And then, one Sunday, you sit down in a pew, and the person you sit beside, who knows your testimony, and knows you came through Teen Challenge, that person promptly gets up and moves to another seat. What do you do about that?"

In each instance, some of the guys would get angry. Reg would say, "Okay, so you're mad. That guy has verbally cut you to pieces, and you're standing there, bleeding on the floor. And you react. Suppose you just shout, 'You dare call me a dirty junkie? Who do you think you are?'

"All he has to do is step back and say, 'Look, folks,' while you're carrying on, 'Look, folks, this guy came out of Teen Challenge. He's supposed to be changed. Why, he isn't changed. He's the same old dirty guy he used to be.' You see, you've been had. He set you up, and he killed you. You would be destroyed and never go back to that church again. And there's a good chance you might not even go on serving the Lord. You might just throw in the sponge. And there are a thousand variations on those three instances."

That would sober the class, and there would be a silence while the reality of it sank in. Then Reg would say, "Here's what you do. First of all, keep your mouth shut, don't say anything. In all of those situations, walk away, because your first instinct will be to react, and if you react, you're in trouble. So the best thing to do is to go home, go to your own place where you can be alone with God, and cry it out to Him. Don't *do* anything for a week, or maybe ten

170

days—because you've dealt with your hurt and your anger in Christ, and you're sure in your own heart that you've got God's solution to it. Then, after waiting, if you feel that God would have you speak to the person, and you are no longer angry, you can confront him with facts."

Reg would close his course on Church Relationships by relating something that happened in his own life when he was new in the ministry and discouraged, at the end of his rope and ready to quit. "I went to talk with an older pastor in Terre Haute, Indiana. He took a strong line with me and told me, 'You will never go higher than you aim.' So I say to each of you: What are you aiming for? If you're aiming to be a ditchdigger, you'll be a ditchdigger. If you're aiming to be a garbage man, you'll be a garbage man. What do you want to be, in Christ? Because, in *Him*, all things are possible."

Then Reg asks them, as their last homework assignment, to write a page, telling what they want to be. "I'm going to read that paper, and then I'm going to put it in your file, and we'll see what the Lord does. But just remember: Teen Challenge is not the program; *Jesus* is the program!"

I was early for the Friday evening service; there were only half a dozen guys in the chapel. In ones and twos, they knelt on the floor and leaned on their folded-down chair seats. I could catch phrases from their prayers—*"Gloria Dios"* . . . "Praise you,

171

Lord."

I took a seat about halfway back, on the aisle, and thought about all that had happened in the last six days. Six days—was it possible? It seemed like six months. And I prayed again the prayer that someone else had prayed my second night here, that God would somehow sort it all out and show me what could be omitted, and what should be brought out.

It was getting on toward seven-thirty, and the chapel was beginning to fill. There would not be the usual crowd of visitors, young people from all over the valley; the roads had drifted over, the temperature was on its way to setting new record lows, and we were snowbound. But the guys were freshly showered and shaved all the same, and wearing their best clothes. I could see where some nice church ladies might indeed have trouble believing their backgrounds.

I looked at the front of the chapel, and for the first time noticed that there were not one but three crosses on the wall behind the pulpit. The three crosses of Calvary, of course—but then the special significance of those three crosses in this particular chapel struck me. The other two crosses were for two felons, men who had come from the same sort of background as many of those now entering the chapel. Each of those two thieves faced certain death of the most excruciating kind, and each had an eleventh-hour opportunity to accept Christ and go on with Him to life immortal. But only one availed himself of the opportunity. That same choice faced each former felon who came into this chapel. And it was a choice that had to be made daily, the choice of the cross-life, of dying out to self and going on in Christ.

The first strains of "Jesus, Jesus, there is something about that name" began to fill the chapel, under the soft, amiable level of conversation. A few people picked up the chorus, then, more, and gradually the guys settled down and joined in. Sammy, who had been scheduled to go home to Harrisburg that night, was at the piano, and two guitarists had plugged their instruments into an amplifier and were trying to get in tune. Next, Sammy swung into, "Oh, How I Love Jesus," and by now everyone was singing. "This is the day the Lord hath made" came next, and a number of guys clapped out a fast double-time rhythm. It was obvious that the guys had sung these songs together many times, and welcomed them as old friends. Circumspectly, I looked around, and noted that there were hardly any guys who weren't singing. Indeed, one would have to be awfully mad at God and everyone else to resist the infectious spirit that pervaded that place.

"I love you, dear Father in Heaven" was the next song, and they sang the second verse in Spanish, "*Yo te amo. . . .*" I had a sense of being in a very large, multilingual family, a family made not by man, but by God. A family, brought together by Him, for growth and healing, with *His* love, vertical and horizontal, and not man's, that made it work.

Sammy stepped to the pulpit and spoke into the microphone. He told the fellows how much he had been counting on going home that weekend, to see his mother—and his girl friend—but he could thank the Lord and give it all up to Him, because this was obviously where he was supposed to be this night. Then he called on each of them to give up the things they were unhappy about or that had crossed their wills, and to trust God with every part of their lives and join in the worship of Him. And judging from the volume of the next song, nearly all present were able to do that.

A family in Christ—these men, learning what it meant to be brothers in Christ. Not as the world understood brothers, brawling and jealous and putting one another down under a veneer of caring. But as Christ intended brothers to live—in honor preferring one another, and caring enough about one another to speak truth when it needed to be spoken, to persevere with each other until they were in the light—in short, living *in* Christ. That was the Jesus factor, and that made all the difference.

DIRECTORY

TEEN CHALLENGE
CENTERS AND OUTREACHES

ALABAMA
Teen Challenge of Birmingham, Inc.
P.O. Box 3626
542 15th Street SW
Birmingham, AL 35211
Dan Delcamp, Director
(205) 780-2094
(Phase I, II, Male Res.)

ARIZONA
Main Office
Teen Challenge of Arizona
P.O. Box 13444
Phoenix, AZ 85002
Snow Peabody, Executive Director
(602) 277-7469

ARKANSAS
Teen Challenge of Arkansas, Inc.
P.O. Box 6056
1701 Center Street
Little Rock, AR 72206
Troy Collier, Director
(501) 376-7191
(Phase I, II, III, Female Res.)

CALIFORNIA (Northern)
Teen Challenge Central Office
P.O. Box 5280

6109 Mac Arthur Blvd.
Oakland, CA 94605
Kenneth D. Shaw, Jr., Business Manager
Dennis Ortega, Director of Evangelism & Development
(415) 562-1141

Teen Challenge Men's Center
San Francisco Center
P.O. Box 40100
1464 Valencia Street
San Francisco, CA 94140
Steve Birdwell, Director
(415) 285-1353
(Phase I, II, III, Male Res.)

Lodi Men's Center
P.O. Box 213
307 W. Lockeford Street
Lodi, CA 95240

(209) 369-2724
(Phase II, III, Male Res.)

Oakland Outreach Center
P.O. Box 5097
6109 Mac Arthur Blvd.
Oakland, CA 94605
Kenneth D. Shaw, Jr., Director
(415) 562-1141
(Phase I)

Gwen Wilkerson Home for Girls
San Jose Center
204 Asbury Street

San Jose, CA 95110
Conrad Cooper, Director
(408) 275-8240
(Phase II, III, Female Res.)

Sacramento Women's Center
P.O. Box 20436
Sacramento, CA 95820
Shirley Hooper, Director
(916) 456-3819
(Phase I, II, III, Female Res.)

CALIFORNIA (Southern)

Main Office
1543 W. Garvey
West Covina, CA 91790
Richard Fort, District Administrator
Jene Wilson, District Director
(213) 962-6787

Bakersfield Teen Challenge
P.O. Box 1011
Bakersfield, CA 93302
Tom Tiemens, Director
(805) 832-4920
(Phase I)

Los Angeles Teen Challenge
2249-63 S. Hobart Blvd.
Los Angeles, CA 90018
Mark Flick, Director
(213) 732-8141
(Phase I, II, Male Res.)

Orange County Teen Challenge
P.O. Box 61
Orange, CA 92666
Ron Bone, Director
(714) 633-3000
(Phase I)

Christian Life School
P.O. Box 5068
Riverside, CA 92507
Glenn Timmons, Director
(714) 683-4241
(Phase III, Male Res.)

San Diego Teen Challenge
7111 El Cajon Blvd.
San Diego, CA 92115
Mike Jackson, Director
(714) 461-9111
(Phase I)

Ventura Teen Challenge
P.O. Box 1064
Ventura, CA 93001
Herb Davis, Director
(805) 643-1244

COLORADO

Teen Challenge of Colorado, Inc.
P.O. Box 1676
Denver, CO 80201
Royce Nimmons, Director
(303) 455-3226
(Phase I, II, III, Male & Female Res.)

FLORIDA

Gulf Coast Teen Challenge
P.O. Box 1044
106 W. Cervantes
Pensacola, FL 32595
Mike Warren, Acting Director
(904) 438-5534
(Phase I, II, Male Res.)

Teen Challenge, Inc.
1124 NW 7th Avenue
Miami, FL 33136

(305) 547-2778
(Phase I, II, Male Res.)

HAWAII
Teen Challenge of Hawaii
Main Office
P.O. Box 434
1178 Fort Street Mall
Honolulu, HI 96809
Don Hall, Executive Director
Hap Pool, Business Administrator
(808) 521-2902

Teen Challenge Oahu
P.O. Box 434
1178 Fort Street Mall
Honolulu, HI 96809
Victor Guzman, Program Coordinator
(808) 521-2902
(Phase I)

Keola Hou Training Center
P.O. Box 1016
Waipahu, HI 96797
Ronald York, Director
(808) 668-8330
(Phase II, III, Male Res.)

The Shaloha House
4670 Kahala Avenue
Honolulu, HI 96816
Tony Wlliams, Director
(808) 734-4951
(Phase II, IV, Female Res.)

Teen Challenge Maui
P.O. Box 725
Wailuku, HI 96793
Orville Sexton, Director
(808) 661-3914
(Phase I, II, III, IV, Male &
Female)

ILLINOIS
Chicago Teen Challenge
315 S. Ashland Avenue
Chicago, IL 60607
(312) 421-0111
(Phase I, II, Male Res.)

Twin City Teen Challenge
108 E. Clark
Champaign, IL 61820
Henry Mohn, Director
(217) 352-6060
(Phase I, II, Male Res.)

INDIANA
Indianapolis Teen Challenge
145 E. Fall Creek Pkwy. S. Drive
Indianapolis, IN 46205
Betty Violette, Director
(317) 924-5463
(Phase I, II, III, Male & Female
Res. under 17 years of age)

KENTUCKY
Teen Challenge of Kentucky, Inc.
P.O. Box 4436
1228 East Broadway
Louisville, KY 40204
Billy Lee Dickey, Director
(502) 583-3155
(Phase I, II, Female Res.)

LOUISIANA
Louisiana Teen Challenge
P.O. Box 52918
1901-1907 Franklin Avenue
New Orleans, LA 70152
Bill Hudson, Director
(504) 949-1659
(Phase I, II, Male Res.)

MARYLAND
Teen Challenge of Maryland
P.O. Box 8937
1806 Tyler Road
Baltimore, MD 21222
David Stewart, Director
(301) 282-6167

Delmarva Teen Challenge
Rehobeth, MD 21857
Dennis Reedy, Director
(301) 957-2990
(Phase II, Male Res.)

MASSACHUSETTS
Teen Challenge of Boston, Inc.
P.O. Box 3265
1315 Main Street
Brockton, MA 02403
Robert Beuscher, Director
(617) 586-1494
(Phase I, II, Male Res.)

MICHIGAN
Detroit Teen Challenge
P.O. Box 10192
11425 S. Telegraph Road
Detroit, MI 48210
Samuel Dobrotka, Director
(313) 287-2970
(Phase I, II, III, Male Res.)

Teen Challenge of Greater Muske-
gon
440 Pontaluna Road
Muskegon, MI 49444
Phillip J. McClain, Director
(616) 798-3788
(Phase I, II, III, Male & Female
Res.)

Teen Challenge of Saginaw, Inc.
Box 1020
Saginaw, MI 48606
Benjamin M. Stowell, Director
(517) 753-1103
(Phase I, II, Male Res.)

MISSISSIPPI
Teen Challenge of Mississippi
P.O. Box 1344
Biloxi, MS 39533
Frank Webb, Director
(601) 435-5469
(Phase I)

MISSOURI
Mid-America Teen Challenge
Training Center
P.O. Box 1089
Oriole Road
Cape Girardeau, MO 63701
Herb Meppelink, Director
(314) 335-6508
(Phase I, III, Male Res.)

Teen Challenge of Greater Kansas
City
25 West 39th Street
Kansas City, MO 64111
James Collier, Director
(816) 753-6600
(Phase I, II, Male Res.)

Teen Challenge of St. Louis
Box 4915
5261 Washington Blvd.
St. Louis, MO 63108
Jack Borth, Director
(314) 367-2225 or 367-2226
(Phase I, II, Male Res.)

NEW YORK

New York Teen Challenge
444 Clinton Avenue
Brooklyn, NY 11238
Don Wilkerson, Director
(212) 789-1414
(Phase I, II, Male Res.)

Camp Champion
Box 89
Glen Spey, NY 12737
(914) 856-3652

The Walter Hoving Home
Box 194
Phillipse Brook & Avery Road
Garrison, NY 10524
John Benton, Director
(914) 424-3674

Teen Challenge of Greater Rochester
P.O. Box 42
75 Alexander Street
Rochester, NY 14601
Herbert Severin, Jr., Director
(716) 325-7123
(Phase I, II, Male Res.)

Teen Challenge of Greater Syracuse
124 Furman Street
Syracuse, NY 13205
Norman Crum, Director
(315) 478-4139
(Phase I, II, Male Res.)

NORTH CAROLINA

Teen Challenge of North Carolina
P.O. Box 1094
Goldsboro, NC 27530

Mrs. Addie Blalock, Director
(919) 736-0656
(Phase I, II, Female Res.)

Greater Piedmont Challenge
Teen Challenge, Inc.
P.O. Box 33
Sedalia, NC 27342
Jerry McAnulty, Director
(919) 449-4622 or 292-0925
(Phase I, II, Male Res.)

OHIO

Teen Challenge of Greater Cleveland
3510 Chester Avenue
Cleveland, OH 44114
Ray Fields, Director
(216) 361-1895 or 951-2893

Teen Challenge Village
3032 Perry Park Road
Perry, OH 44077
Neal McFarland, Supervisor
(216) 259-3333
(Phase II, III, Male Res.)

Greater Cincinnati Teen Challenge
(216) 361-1895 or 951-2893
1410 Vine Street
Cincinnati, OH 45214
James C. Gray, Director
(513) 721-5755 or 721-5435
(Phase I, II, Male Res.)

Columbus Teen Challenge
47 E. 12th Avenue
Columbus, OH 43201
Larry Stitt, Director
(614) 294-5331
(Phase I, III, Female Res.)

PENNSYLVANIA

Teen Challenge of Greater
Philadelphia Inc.
1620 N. Broad Street
Philadelphia, PA 19121
(215) 232-4636

Teen Challenge Training Center
Box 98
Rehrersburg, PA 19550
Reg Yake, Director
(717) 933-4181 or 933-8694
(Phase III, Male Res.)

Harrisburg Teen Challenge
1421 N. Front Street
Harrisburg, PA 17102
Lou Demmi, Director
(717) 233-6549
(Phase I, II, Male Res.)

PUERTO RICO

Teen Challenge de Puerto Rico,
Inc.
Box 4273
Bayamon Gardens Station
Bayamon, PR 00619
Jaime Perez, Director
(809) 783-0522
(Phase I, II, Male Res.)

TENNESSEE

Teen Challenge of Memphis
P.O. Box 22363
3519 Douglas Avenue
Memphis, TN 38122
Tim Waters, Director
(901) 452-8541
(Phase I)

TEXAS (North)

Austin Teen Challenge
P.O. Box 13021
1210 Nueces, Suite 210
Austin, TX 78711
Jackson Boyett, Director
(512) 472-6351 or 441-3656
(Phase I)

Dallas Teen Challenge
P.O. Box 26112
703 S. Beacon
Dallas, TX 75226
Lyle Noah, Director
(214) 824-6181
(Phase I, II, Male Res.)

Boys' Dormitory
5119 Garland Avenue
Dallas, TX 75223
Jerry Holley, Director

Teen Challenge of Fort Worth
P.O. Box 731
747 Samuels Avenue
Fort Worth, TX 76101
Larry Adley, Director
(817) 336-8191
(Phase I, II, Female Res.)

Teen Challenge
P.O. Box 1165
114 S. Broadway
Tyler, TX 75701
Joe Fauss, Director
(214) 597-6111
(Phase I, II, Male & Female Res.)

TEXAS (South)

Houston Teen Challenge
P.O. Box 1451

411 Westheimer
Houston, TX 77001
David Kirschke, Director
(713) 526-5660 or 526-5669
(Phase I, IV)
(Phase II for girls over 18)
(Phase II for men over 26)

San Antonio Teen Challenge
P.O. Box 2242
2143 South W.W. White
San Antonio, TX 78206
Ronald Woodcock, Director
(512) 223-5859
(Phase I)

Westwood Farm
Route 3 Box 61
Floresville, TX 78114
Robert W. Rutherford, Director
(512) 393-6762
(Phase I, II, Male Res.)

TEXAS (West)

Teen Challenge of West Texas
2200 San Jose
El Paso, TX 79930
Hector Ruiz, Director
(915) 565-0300
(Phase I, II, Female Res.)

West Texas Teen Challenge
P.O. Box 251
201 "C" Street
Midland, TX 79701
Chuck Redger, Director
(915) 682-3244
(Phase I, II, Male Res.)

WASHINGTON

Northwest Teen Challenge

1808 18th Avenue
Seattle, WA 98122
David Torres, Director
(206) 324-3560
(Phase I, II, III, Male & Female
Res.)

Teen Challenge Drug Center
Box 1302
Lewiston, ID 83501
Hank Hebard, Area Director
(208) 746-3084

Longview Teen Challenge
P.O. Box 695
Longview, WA 98632
Brent Ebinger, Area Director
(206) 577-0200

Teen Challenge
P.O. Box 5396
Vancouver, WA 98663
Paul Salgado, Area Director
(206) 256-0700

Aberdeen Outreach Cof-
feehouse
P.O. Box 449
Aberdeen, WA 98520
(206) 532-6211
(Phase I)

WASHINGTON, D.C.

Teen Challenge of
Washington D.C.
P.O. Box 6165
812 Fifth Street NW
Washington, DC 20044
Michael Zello, Director
(202) 347-0404
(Phase I, II, Male Res.)

183

This chapter has been added to better acquaint you with your local Teen Challenge program.

TEEN CHALLENGE
IN CINCINNATI

The sirens screamed and the flashing lights cut through the rain and darkness as the squad cars from the District 1 Police Department scurried to the corner of 13th and Vine. The gang fight which had been in full swing moments earlier was over almost as quickly as it had started. With the first wail of the sirens, two dozen teen-age guys and girls had run in all directions. Two teen-age boys and a girl who had lingered behind were shoved briskly into a paddy wagon. Another boy lay face down on the sidewalk in a pool of blood, a switchblade protruding from his back. For the many winos and drug addicts in this Over-The-Rhine bar district of Cincinnati, it was just another night on Vine Street. But for the young news reporter, Ken Bagwell, it was a night never to be forgotten. After phoning his story to the Al Schottlecotte News Service where he worked, Ken called it a night and headed for home. He spent the next several days with a strange inward desire to do something for those kids who were locked into a life of crime and drugs. Again and again the thought crossed his mind, "Someone needs to do something to help . . . someone *must* do something!"

Ken's burden to help those kids became so great that he was heard to say, "I would give my life to help those kids if necessary." And so it was that in September of 1972 that Ken and his wife Jody began to walk the ghetto streets sharing the love of Jesus Christ with anyone who would care to listen. As Ken and Jody shared their burden for these youth with friends, they were soon joined by a handful of others who also had been strangely moved to "do something" to help. Among these workers was a local TV personality, Len Mink, whom Ken had led to the Lord while working as associate producer of his show. Now he and his wife Cathy were busy helping Ken to win others to Jesus. A short time later God broke another heart over the needs of this city and Jim Gray, the current Teen Challenge director, became a permanent part of Ken's group of workers.

This small group began to walk the ghetto streets and frequent the teen hangouts in hopes of picking up the "pulse beat" of the city. A "pulse beat" that seemed to say again and again, "We have lost our way, could you please help us?" There were literally hundreds of teen-agers in the city who were desperately in need of help as a result of drug and alcohol addiction. Over six thousand hard-core heroin addicts were known to have been in treatment at various methadone clinics and the police narcotics division evaluated the drug problem as "critical." Other statistics showed that drugs and crime were doing their lethal work in our city as every available detention facility was filled to capacity. More than twenty-five thousand youth had gone through the juvenile court system the previous year.

the group drew faith from the proven success of the Teen Challenge ministry over the past fourteen years on the streets of New York City. Each time they asked, "What can we do?" the answer seemed to come back—"A Teen Challenge ministry must be established right here in Cincinnati!" This seemed impossible. Not one person in the group of workers had ever been hooked on drugs and knew very little about working with addicts. An even greater obstacle was the thousands of dollars that would be needed to purchase a building where addicts could live and receive help over an extended period of time. It would indeed take a miracle!

Each day the group would meet for prayer and then walk the dirty streets sharing God's love with all who would listen. Every noon hour seemed to find them sitting on the steps of an old church building at 1410 Vine Street refreshing themselves with Coneys and Coca-Cola. Little did they know that this same century-old building would become the Cincinnati Teen Challenge Center in a few short months.

After looking at every available building in the

area, this one was decided upon as it was situated right in the middle of the action. The asking price of $35,000 seemed totally out of reach but God moved upon several local pastors to put their names on the line and the building was purchased in July of 1973.

Ken Bagwell was appointed director and Jim Gray, his assistant. Jody Bagwell served as secretary and Mike Templin was the outreach counselor. The full-time staff had now leveled off to four as Cathy Mink had been called to a nationwide evangelistic ministry. The staff went to work renovating the building and helping people in need wherever God opened the doors.

One of the first ministries started was the "Kids' Klub" where Bible studies and crafts were taught to the ghetto children. Next came the opportunity to share Christ weekly in the girls' division at the Cincinnati Correctional Institution, where many girls had a life-changing experience through a personal encounter with Jesus Christ. Upon their release, those desiring to go through the program are referred to the Teen Challenge girls' home in Columbus.

Then the most productive door opened when the warden of the Hamilton County Jail asked Ken and Jim to be the chaplains at the jail. They had agreed in prayer that God would somehow help them to reach the three hundred men who were kept there daily. The word quickly spread throughout the jail that "Jesus Christ was changing lives and setting drug addicts free."

Meanwhile over at 1410 Vine Street, work continued on the building by staff and volunteers and it was only a matter of time until the building would be ready for the first boy—or would it be a girl? The answer to this question of whether the ministry would serve boys or girls had been left up to God and on February 15th, 1974, He answered that question. The phone had rung the previous day and the State probation department asked Ken to help a young boy who was addicted to heroin. At 2 P.M. the next day the facility at 1410 Vine Street officially became a Teen Challenge Induction Center as this young man was inducted into the program.

Within two weeks the home was "wall to wall" with young fellows seeking help. The next six weeks proved to be exciting for the staff as they watched their many weeks of labor bring forth fruit in the lives of these young men.

Then on April 14th, 1974, tragedy struck. It was on that Easter eve that Ken Bagwell was attacked by a teen-age boy and beaten severely. Ken suffered injuries that night that were to hospitalize him for the next two years and would finally take his life in May of 1976. At first it seemed as if the infant ministry might be stricken down with its beloved leader. Brokenhearted staff members and friends fought back that inevitable question, "Why him, God?"

The next two years would prove to be times of great trial, yet times of great victory and blessings. Ken's staff and friends were determined to see that the ministry he had founded would continue.

The city that had been blessed by such a ministry as Teen Challenge now in turn began to bless that ministry. The Sycamore-Deer Park Jaycees paid off the $25,000 mortgage balance on the Teen Challenge Center with proceeds from the WSAI Haunted House project while over eighteen hundred people in Cincinnati and across America sent in donations totaling $60,000 to pay Ken's hospital bills.

In the midst of recurring doubts and fears, it seemed that God confirmed again and again that this ministry was ordained to grow and prosper. God in His infinite wisdom chose to use Ken Bagwell's injury and death to bring attention to the ministry which he had founded. Ken had fulfilled his mission and was taken home to be with the Lord, yet his ministry to troubled youth would live on.

As the people began to do their part by supporting this ministry financially, God certainly proved himself faithful by setting drug addicts free at the Teen Challenge Center. Great success was wrought as dozens of lives were changed through faith in Jesus Christ. Some of the first boys that Ken inducted in February of 1974 are on the Teen Challenge staff today, while others are in various Bible schools studying for the ministry. All of the outreach programs that were started in 1972, and 1973 continue to be very productive today and new programs have been added.

The success of the Teen Challenge ministry in

Cincinnati has been so great that it has outgrown its facility of 1410 Vine Street. Last year alone over five thousand young men and women were ministered to on the streets and in the various jails of the city. Dozens of boys were inducted into the local program while over thirty others were placed in various Teen Challenge facilities in other cities. Almost daily, youth were turned away due to the shortage of space. Staff and concerned friends began to pray for a place to build. Again God answered prayer in a very definite way and a ninety-eight-acre farm was practically given to the Teen Challenge ministry by a local physician, Lee Davidson.

Dozens of Teen Challenge supporters recently walked up the hill at the farm to participate in ground-breaking ceremonies for the new "Kenneth Bagwell Home for Boys." This $200,000 project will enable the ministry to triple its capacity. Students will no longer have to be sent to the farm at Rehrersburg but will be kept at this facility for the full year program. The long-range plans for the farm include a vocational program to teach the students work skills for which volunteer teachers are being screened. The Teen Challenge staff feel this must be a priority as almost every boy that comes to the program is a junior high dropout. They feel that it is not enough just to help youth become drug free, but they must be equipped to reenter society as productive citizens. The philosophy of Teen Challenge is to "reach the total man totally" and it is our goal to develop the Teen Challenge farm into a

Christian community where shattered lives can be put together piece by piece.

The following testimonies by two of our graduates speak more graphically of the work Ken Bagwell started in Cincinnati than could anything else we might say.

David Leopold

I started out just like everyone else, I guess, drinking a little beer and getting a little high on the weekends. I hardly ever got out of the neighborhood because there was no reason to—all my friends, including my girl friend, lived close to me. When I was fifteen, I began to drink more and more—before school and after school, almost every day. As I blindly persisted in this my girl friend, who was almost the whole world to me, broke up with me. From that day on I really began to change for the worse and began to hang round with a different group of people. I started smoking pot to forget about my girl and the other things I didn't want to remember.

I started doing more drugs and losing interest in everything, including school, home life, people, and my self-respect. I didn't know it then, but I was getting blinder and blinder. A friend of mine was thrown out of his house and he came to live at my house for a while. We both liked to get high a lot, so we began to do more of it—even while at school. One day my friend was rolling a joint in biology class and he got caught. He was taken to the principal's office and, when I heard about it, my natural reaction was to help my friend out. The principal refused to talk with me and we got in a fight. All I got for my trouble was a bad reputation at the school and, eventually, I was kicked out of Milford schools for good. When that happened, I thought I was free.

Before I knew it, I had developed a drug habit. I needed cash to support my habit and so I lied to my parents about needing a job to buy a car. Instead of repaying my parents for the car, I spent my paychecks on drugs and my habit continued to grow. During the week I stole money from the cash register where I worked. It was easy. All I had to do was take the money off the readings to balance for the day.

My activities led to several arrests by the state and local police on various charges. Several car accidents in the few months that I had the car provided me with several thousands of dollars from my insurance company. Then my insurance went up so high I canceled it and used the premium money to feed my growing habit. Meanwhile, the Milford police barred my car from the city limits.

By now I was into mind-expanding drugs, like acid and speed. When I shot my first speed, I loved it but as I began to do more and more my mind began to really get messed up. Doing so many drugs and staying high all the time opened up the door for

Satan in my life. It seemed that I was passing through a wall—the wall that separates the kingdom of God and the kingdom of Satan. I don't think many people know about this wall because the people that do pass through it go through so gradually that they don't even notice it. But I went through this wall so fast, and the changes came about so rapidly that it was impossible for me to miss it. Even though I had been brought up in a Christian home and knew God was real, I now had begun to learn that Satan was real, also. My life was filled more and more with Satan's spirit as I journeyed farther into his kingdom and ultimately into Satan worship.

For a solid year I was in a state of confusion and paranoia. I had some frightening experiences with Satan that I still can hardly believe really happened, but they did. The more I got high, the more Satan would come into me. It doesn't work that way with everybody who does drugs, but it did with me.

Christmas eve of 1973 I dropped a couple hits of acid and a couple hits of mescaline and completely lost control of myself. That night I was filled with the spirit of Satan like never before. I will never forget the terrible experiences I had in my room that night. I went completely out of my head. I had dropped so many hits of acid that I couldn't come down. I knew I was on one of those permanent acid trips I had heard so much about, and I prayed that night, for the first time in years, for God to please help me.

I could never explain the way I felt, but one thing I do know, the Spirit of God came on me, put me to sleep and when I woke up I was all right. That was my last acid trip, but I now had a drug habit that I couldn't kick even though I had gotten to the place where I couldn't even smoke pot without Satan coming in full strength. I knew that I was getting deeper into the devil's kingdom, but I was bound by his powers and I couldn't get out. I knew if I didn't do something soon, I would be permanently filled with his spirit—high or not high.

Being filled with this evil spirit was like taking all the hatred, jealousy, paranoia, nervousness and pride in the world and putting it all inside of me until that was all that could come out. I hated every minute of it, but it was too late now because I was in bondage to Satan. One night about nine o'clock, I got a sudden urge to go up to my mom and dad's house. This was very strange because I had spent very little time there in the past year and when I did go home I always slipped in late at night. I couldn't figure it out but decided to go home. When I got there, Jim Gray, executive director of Cincinnati Teen Challenge was there talking to my parents about me.

Jim and I talked alone for a while, and he asked me if I might like to come down to Teen Challenge and check out the program. I knew from that moment God had opened the door for me. I was definitely ready and said yes.

It didn't take long for me to see that Teen Challenge was for me! Every person there was full of the love of Jesus. I knew that this was the real thing and that I had to have it, too.

All I had to do was tell the Lord and choose. And when I did, I watched a miracle take place in my life. All the hatred, jealousy, paranoia and deep things of Satan that were in me—the drugs, cigarettes and booze—left in a split second to make room for the Spirit of God.

I was in the Teen Challenge program for six months and came to know Jesus Christ as my Lord and Savior. He filled me with His Holy Spirit and gave me real love for people. Jesus filled me so full of His joy that I can't hold it in. There is no doubt in my mind that Jesus Christ is the one that did this for me and He hasn't stopped yet. He continues to fill me with His Spirit and teaches me new things every day. Many of my friends have also come to know Him as a result of the change they saw in me. Each passing day gets more exciting as I watch the changes in my life and the people around me. If Jesus Christ can do this for me, I know He can change anyone who will open their heart to Him and give Him a chance.

David is presently a staff member at the Cincinnati Teen Challenge Center. He is happily married and the father of a brand-new son.

Paul Moehring

The first thirteen years of my life I obeyed my parents and the church. But even then I realized there was an emptiness in my life and in the people's lives around me. Although there were people who said they loved me, I never really felt that love. I wanted to find people who loved me and a place where I could be accepted. In 1960 I began to hang around with some older guys and girls. They introduced me to drinking, drugs and fighting. I tried to outdo everyone else in each of these and I really thought I was a part of something.

For the next five years, I struggled through life trying to tell myself that I was having a good time and that my friends loved me. Then, in 1965, I received a call from the army and thought. "Here is my big opportunity. I can start all over." I knew I was headed down the wrong road. But even in the army the desire to be accepted surfaced and my time in the service consisted of organizing a drug ring in Vietnam where almost two-thirds of the soldiers were on dope. I returned from Vietnam with a drug habit so expensive that I couldn't afford it. I got in contact with some people that I had been with in Vietnam and went to work for some men in California and Texas transporting drugs around the country. Once again I thought I was a part of something.

By 1970 I had been in jails coast to coast and the people I worked for were also in jail, so I had to start stealing to support my habit. And my habit grew—the more I stole, the more I needed. That emptiness inside had become so big that no amount of heroin could fill it. I wanted to start over so I tried kicking my habit but the more I tried to kick it, the more heroin I'd shoot. I wanted help but couldn't find anything that worked. Drug programs failed and doctors failed. And as I looked around, I saw that I was abusing everyone who was trying to help me. Finally it got so bad that every time I shot dope, I wanted to die. I remember a lot of times when I was pulling a robbery I wished that some of my victims would catch me and kill me. Life had no meaning . . . no love . . . nothing. I thought, "If I have to spend the rest of my life like this, I might as well be dead."

Finally, in 1975, after fifteen years of drug addiction and twenty convictions for various crimes, I surrendered. Sitting in the county jail with charges that could keep me in prison the rest of my life, a Teen Challenge worker told me that Jesus Christ had died for sinners like me. I cried out to God to help me through everything. Through God's mercy and love, He showed me that I could start over and have a new life—one with meaning and direction. God performed a miracle and I was permitted to come to Teen Challenge. Once here I found what I had been seeking all my life—people who loved me and accepted me as I was.

It has been close to two years since I met Jesus and He keeps getting sweeter and sweeter. Now I am working for the Lord and Teen Challenge trying to show people that they don't have to go through what I did. The fact that I am now a part of our jail ministry is a miracle in itself. I thank God for Teen challenge and His obedient children who support Teen Challenge. I personally would like to thank you all right now for your help in making Teen Challenge available to me and my brothers here. God is good and still changing lives.

Paul works today at the Cincinnati Teen Challenge Center as a staff counselor and pre-admission interviewer for the jail outreach program.

If you would like a representative from the Cincinnati Teen Challenge Center to come to your church or civic group with a film or testimony by an ex-addict, please call or write:

Cincinnati Teen Challenge, Inc.
P.O. Box 14503, 1410 Vine Street
Cincinnati, Ohio 45214

Phone: (513) 721-5755

Teen Challenge

☐ I need help. (please give details) _____

☐ Male   AGE   ☐ under 16   ☐ 23-30

☐ Female   ☐ 17-22   ☐ 30 and over

☐ Please send literature that will help me.

Name _____

Address _____

City _____ State _____ Zip _____